Ken's Greatest Challenge Part 2

THE GUESTBOOK

MICKIE KELLY

ISBN 979-8-88751-136-8 (paperback)
ISBN 979-8-88751-138-2 (digital)

Christian Faith Publishing
832 Park Avenue
Meadville, PA 16335
www.christianfaithpublishing.com

Printed in the United States of America

Preface

During the five-year diary of *Ken's Greatest Challenge* so many of his family, friends, coworkers, students, those that knew him and those that knew about him wrote back to Ken in his Caring Bridge Guestbook. There are many, many encouragements of very inspirational and heartfelt messages. Ken read all of them and appreciated them all so very, very much. I thank you all from the depths of my heart as to what it did to encourage this amazing man.

Ken Kelly, this too is my gift to you, your life and your amazing legacy!

Love, Mickie

Here are some excerpts to get you started:

You are an amazing man and don't deserve this huge "challenge" in your life but God and the universe work in funny ways. Your challenge is teaching humility, strength, love and support to the rest of us who love and care about you. Thank you for being *you*! You are walking in strong, happy footsteps of your mother and you're making us all prouder than we have ever been. Please keep the love and positive outlook always in your heart.

You continue to awe and inspire me as you fight and stand up against the beast. Even as you deal with the tendrils that continue to try and reach out, you continue to hold a perspective towards bettering mankind. You, Sir, are a very strong man. My hope is that, as you stated, your fight will become a benefit to others. You continue to be an inspiration to many, myself included.

Because of you I want to be a better person. I want to help just a fraction of the people you have helped. You are truly an amazing man and one I am honored to know. I now see life in a different way because of your journey and your words.

The way you wear your heart on your sleeve helps me understand more and more each day how precious life is and how important it is to embrace the smallest (which turn out to be the largest) things. I listen to you as you take us all on this journey with you and you end up giving us all strength and a better understanding of just how strong people can be with a little faith, some good friends and a great family.

I am honored to be in your life and to have the opportunity to accompany you on this journey, as dismal as it seems at time. God does not give us challenges we cannot handle. For with faith, love, thanksgiving and the Lord's guidance and blessing, we can handle anything He gives us. While we may never know why these challenges are given to us, I think all of us who are faithful can understand that they make us stronger servants of the Lord.

You my friend have made one of the greatest gifts possible to this earth. You have educated, you have ensured that through your work mankind has been made better. If we all could live to that standard, imagine what life would be like.

May 23rd, 2009

Hey, Dude, I am so glad that we got to see you last week. I always look forward to seeing you when you are in my neck of the woods. It was great to read about the latest news from your oncologist. That really is great to hear. You are a man of strength, wisdom and fortitude. I know that with your strength and faith, you will be able to stare this thing straight in the face and then kick its butt!

As I have said before, I will always be here for you. Whatever you may need, please do not hesitate to call me. You are in my thoughts daily and know that we are praying for you.

Stay in touch and God bless.

K. T. and Family

May 23rd, 2009

Hi Kenny, I want to send you a big hug and let you know I also believe that you will stare this nastiness down. I love you, Cuz. You are the most positive and fiercely optimistic man I know. That is how it's done.

Love,
J. F. F.

May 26th, 2009

Hi Kenny. I am so glad that you have this website to keep us all in touch. Where did the time go? Where did the years slip away? How did that happen so fast? Why does it take something painful to re-remind us of how special we all are and give us that wake-up call again?

Please know that I am sending you lots of loving prayers, blessings and thank yous for being you and being such an incredible person.

I remember when we were kids coming out to Lima (or the "boonies") to visit you all and spend the day and have family fun and family times. We would play and eat together. Sundays, weekends and holidays were always special family times like parents, kids and families just don't seem to have the time to do today. You guys always lived out there in the wide-open spaces with so much to explore that doesn't seem to exist much anymore. You *all* are special, and I love you all.

All those old sayings we heard our grandparents say and we pooh-poohed make sense now, don't they? The older you get, the smarter you get…too soon you get old, too late you get smart… time and life are short…they go on and on. Funny how they make so much sense now, don't they?

I am so very grateful for all the love and family connections we have and have had—even though we've gotten lax or caught up in life since our moms, dads and uncles are not here. I hope and pray that we will continue throughout the years, even though it seems to have slipped away with time and everyone being "so very busy with life, kids, family, stuff and all".

You have always been special and especially special when you stood up and took charge and helped out when you suddenly had to become the man of the family and comforted your mom. You, my cousin, are wonderful and special. You have always been there with your mom, God bless her soul. What an amazing woman she was, and what an amazing man you have turned out to be. God bless you in everything, and I thank you for all of that.

I hope we can all get together while I am visiting and helping out in the garden through June 10th. I am looking forward to it, and also, I'll be home in August and Christmas. Home is, and always will be, where the heart is and where your roots are.

Much love coming your way always,
K. L. H.

May 27th, 2009

What can I say (yes, I know…me at a loss for words?) except, *you are a strong person who will make all efforts to overcome*! You have not only taught in EMS (emergency medical services), you cared for EMS! That's what makes you a person who not only cared for the EMS people but also the EMS families. Stay cool.

D. R.

May 27th, 2009

Ken, I don't know where I would be in life if it wasn't for you taking me under your wing and showing me what I was truly able to do in life. You will always be more than a boss and teacher to me. You will always be a true friend of mine and I'm proud to call you that. I know you are a strong person and you will beat this. Keep in touch and I hope to see you September 26th, 2009, at my wedding.

K. G. (F.)

May 27th, 2009

Ken, you and Mickie are amazing people and would give anyone the shirt off your back if needed. You have mentored and taught so many people your gift of Paramedicine. You, and a few others, have pushed and molded my husband into the paramedic he is today and for that I thank you from the bottom of my heart. Who knows, maybe one day you could see him teaching. You never know. You are a fighter and a strong person who I know won't give up unless you truly believe that nothing else can be done, but I also know that you won't just sit around. You are the type of person who lives life to the fullest. So I wish you the best. Stay strong. If you need anything at all, please don't hesitate to ask, even if it's just boring our son for a day to have fun. Trust me, he'll keep you on your toes.

All our love,
J., M., D. and M. B.

May 27th, 2009

To you, Ken, and your family, all the best wishes.

R. B.

May 27th, 2009

Ken, it sorrows me to hear of your newest and greatest challenge. You are a strong person who will meet this challenge head on. And no matter the outcome, it is a win-win. You either spend more time here with those you love…or you enter into the presence of our Lord and help prepare our place there.

Your contribution to our profession is mountainous. Those you have taught and mentored carry on the excellence of their teacher, and hopefully, they will share that knowledge with others who will continue.

You and your loved ones are in my prayers as you meet this challenge together. *May the Lord bless you and keep you. May the Lord lift up His face upon you. May the Lord keep you in His favor and grant you peace.*

R. Z.

May 27th, 2009

You have had many challenges before and you have certainly helped me with mine. You and Mickie are in my prayers as you face the challenges ahead. You asked me who my hero was and that we shared the same hero, B. L., but now I have a new hero, and that is you. Thank you for all that you have taught me and believe me, it is more than just emergency medicine. If I can help in anyway, just ask.

E. Z. (Y.)

May 27th, 2009

Hi Ken and Mickie! A little birdie broke the news to me a little while ago, and F. and I were in shock. Thank you for providing this opportunity to all of us to support you and offer words of encouragement.

I have to tell you, when I heard about FLA (Finger Lakes Ambulance), the better protocols, from J., I just had to come out there. I was at that point where I was getting "crispy" at my other five jobs and honestly wanted to stop being a paramedic and start a new chapter. After meeting you and coming out to FLA, I felt like that new paramedic again, learning more stuff, having fun; and I started to enjoy life again. I enjoyed it so much that I quit all my other jobs and for the first time in twelve years of EMS, I had *one job*! It was awesome. You made it awesome. I had someone to look up to that wasn't an idiot or on a power trip. You and Mickie always made me smile and feel welcomed. I never expected a knee injury would take me out of the career I figured I'd be working in for the next three or four decades. Because of you, I was able to gracefully leave EMS (although not by my choosing) and have wonderful and fond memories of how great it is and how it gets in your blood and doesn't leave. For that, I cannot thank you enough, Mr. Kelly.

People have expressed many of the same thoughts and feelings that F. and I share. You have made New York a much better and safer place to be. Your spirit will carry on through the rest of us, and I hope that helps ease your mind. I know you will meet this challenge like a multivehicle crash with a tractor trailer, an MCI (mass casualty incident), head on with precision and a bit of soft gentle grace that is the swagger of Ken Kelly.

In typical B. J. fashion, here's a stab at making you laugh, knowing that no equipment was broken in the process will hopefully bring a smile to your handsome face:

One wintry night, not too long after I started at FLA, one of the ambulances had an unexpected encounter with the train tracks in the city of Geneva. I'm thinking this is a decent time to come clean, as I'm sure by now you may have heard a rumor about a rig stuck on the train tracks. Sir, it was I! I turned down what I thought was a back alley because I had pulled a practical joke on the other crew and they were looking for us. In my attempt to hide the giant billboard (also known as a Finger Lakes Ambulance), I ended up doing a bit of off-roading. Once I realized where I was, I attempted to leave the area, and with that bus, I slid on the wet snow and ice. The two wheels went over the tracks, and we were stuck! Many attempts were made to extricate ourselves from the mess I had created, and with the help of the other crew, the bus was literally picked up and moved off the tracks. I am sorry I never admitted to this debacle until now (*grin*), but it feels appropriate since I just got a job in the real world and my EMS career is a fond memory that I can draw upon. Angels were with us that night as the train did not come through on time and I didn't have to explain why my bus was on the tracks to begin with and, oh yeah, we need a new ambulance and all the equipment that goes with it because a train obliterated the rig!

I need to thank you for giving me my life back. With your encouragement, with the whole weight-loss challenge, you put hope into my life that I would one day loose some weight. Part of the pain with my knee injury was because I was a fat butt. I didn't want to let you down. I wanted to loose weight. For the first time, I really tried to loose and for the first time, I won. I finally have a regular schedule, can cook and sleeping six to seven hours instead of two to three. To date, I have lost sixty pounds and Monday, I bought my first sized 14/16 shirt (I was in a size 24) and my pants went from size 56 to a

42! I have a few more to go, but if it wasn't for you, I would never have started. Ken, you've been my hero and inspiration for the past year. You gave me my life back in multiple ways. *Thank you!* My knee pain is diminishing, and I'm hoping to get another motorcycle next spring. We should go riding!

I like angels too. I believe in them, and I believe in you. You'll meet this challenge like a seasoned paramedic and have it wondering who the heck did it mess with. You're one of the best and I'm not just saying that. I will be thinking of you guys often, and I will do whatever to help you in any way.

B. J. O.

May 27ᵗʰ, 2009

Ken and Mickie, thanks for taking the time, effort and energy to develop this website. The site will give others an opportunity to be of support to you without feeling that we are invading your privacy. You will remain in my thoughts and prayers. Let the angels ride strong and let us all pray that they do their work.

L. R. T.

May 27ᵗʰ, 2009

Ken, just a quick hi and I'll see you at work, so no need for lots of talk here.

B. C.

May 27ᵗʰ, 2009

Mr. Kelly—I cannot address you as Ken, it just doesn't seem to give sufficient respect—I am writing because A. is not as proficient at speaking her feelings. I am the writer in the family.

7

I would like to thank you for creating the amazing individual A. has become. You have taught her that she can be anything she wishes to be. You have guided her through her difficult times and understood even when personal things interfered with her work. I am incredibly proud of the paramedic that she is, and you are directly responsible for that.

I would also like to offer you some alternative medicine. I am sure, if you are not knowledgeable of it, you will do the research! A. and myself are Reiki practitioners. It can't hurt you, but it surely does help. If nothing else, it can help reduce the pain. Feel free to contact me if you are not comfortable contacting A. We are at your disposal.

Our prayers and healing energies are with you. You may just hear from me again sometime.

C. D., A. K.'s "Other Supervisor"!

May 27th, 2009

Ken, I am sorry to hear of your most recent challenge. You are in my thoughts and prayers. You have touched so many lives and I know you will continue to do so in the future.

L. R.

May 27th, 2009

Mr. Kelly, what can I say that hasn't already been said by so many? You are an amazing man. You believed in me when most didn't, when even I didn't. You have molded so many of us into what we are today. Sometimes I wonder if you have any idea what a profound impact you have made to so many. I know that, personally, you helped me to see life from an entirely new perspective. You made me realize that I am in control of my life and who I am. It is thanks to you that my children and I are where we are today. You have been the biggest influence in my life. Whenever I get the strength to fight something impossible, I think of you, and I always will.

Thank you. Thank you so much for being my mentor, my boss, my instructor and the person who I respect most.

Love,
C. B.

May 27ᵗʰ, 2009

Ken, it is so hard to hear bad news about the people you care for and love. I know that we truly don't have a connection; but I feel, through K., we have a wonderful friendship. He speaks so highly of you and respects you so much. We both know in our hearts that you will beat this, and we would love to be there and help out the best we can. You have made K. into the person, the paramedic, the father and the soon-to-be husband that he is today. I wish you the best of luck. If you need anything, please contact us. I know you will overcome this and one day you will teach M. to be a great paramedic, just like her daddy.

Lots of love from all of us!

P. and K. G.

May 27ᵗʰ, 2009

Mr. Kelly, Sir, I can't remember when I didn't call you that at least once a day. Sometimes Ken, but always with respect. This coming from a man who is how many years older than you? Growing up in a military family might just have had something to do with it. What do you think?

When I first heard the news, about this latest challenge you were facing, I felt saddened. As the information began to sink in, it dawned on me that you are a man of faith, with strong convictions, and was reminded of scripture that says, "*I can do all things through Christ (God) who strengthens me*". Not very good at quoting the Bible, yet I think you know what scripture I am attempting to quote. When faced with my personal battle with cancer, my pastor gave

9

me a bracelet that I still wear almost three years later, "God Strong, Ephesians 6:10–11". It has helped not only with my fight with this dreaded disease, but also in getting through a few more struggles. For instance, your most recent paramedic class and passing the state exam. You have that faith that is needed to face this challenge and to beat its butt!

Three short years ago, I was a greenhorn Basic EMT (emergency medical technician), so wet behind the ears that it was almost comical. Now I am a greenhorn paramedic, still wet behind the ears, with so much more to learn. Yet all made somewhat easier because you believed in me and helped me believe in myself. For that I am privileged and honored to work not only for you, but with you.

You make a difference every day in the lives of the people you care for in the back of an ambulance. Also, the people you instruct in the numerous classes you teach and the people who work with you as well as countless others. I have faith that you will continue to do so.

I have a great idea—let's be old paramedics together! God bless you and Mickie. You both are in our prayers.

R. T.

May 27th, 2009

God bless you and your family! Be as strong as you've taught others to be!

A. D.

May 27th, 2009

My sweet friend Ken, I have so much to say to you and while you and I never need words, I'm going to just write just a few of them. So when I moved to Canandaigua in 1994, I met the love of my life and your best friend. Who knew I would be blessed with you in that deal? You have been so important to me and I have to thank you. Your friendship, support, love, humor, generosity, knowledge and living example are what define you. Please let me share with you a few inspirational thoughts. You *must* fight! You *must* lean on your family and friends! You *must* rebuke negativity and embrace optimism! Most importantly, and I mean this from the bottom of my heart, you *must* remember that *nobody* loves you like D. does. Also J. and I love you too.

L. Y.

May 27th, 2009

Ken, "*May the Lord bless you and keep you. The Lord make His face shine upon you and be gracious to you. The Lord turn His face towards you and give you peace*" (Numbers 6:24–26). Find strength in our Lord Jesus Christ for He is all holy. May He look down upon you and give you the strength and courage needed to face the challenges ahead. Be strong, knowing you are well loved and respected by all you have touched. Do not go quietly into the night. Live well and be happy! Smile often, though the skies may be dark. Every day is a new beginning. Take it and run!

God bless you, Ken Kelly! Be strong. Be well.

J. D. #110

May 28th, 2009

Colonel Kelly, I am sorry and saddened to learn of your "greatest challenge". What can I say that hasn't been said by so many others?

I would just like to say thank you. Thank you for being my friend and a wonderful boss back in the day of the original crew at Finger Lakes Ambulance.

You, Mickie, and family will be in my thoughts and prayers. If there is ever a time when you need anything, please call. Continue to keep your trust and faith in God and stay strong.

The original Dinger, LOL, #188, D. D.

May 28th, 2009

    Mr. Kelly, I haven't been at FLA for very long, but in the short year, my outlook on EMS and life in general has changed so much. You have been there for so many people and done so much. I know you were disappointed that I didn't go through with my paramedic class this year, but I want you to know that I plan on continuing with that plan in a year or so. At first, I was scared to talk to you, but after one really bad call, you were right there to talk and to lend a lot of encouragement and advice, and I will never forget that. I have known Mickie for going on seven years now. You two are both wonderful people and you will be in my thoughts and prayers! Stay strong and allow yourself to lean on others as we have so had to lean on you.

C. J.

May 28th, 2009

    Ken, you were my first EMT instructor, my Crew Chief at CES (Canandaigua Emergency Squad) and my friend. I enjoyed working with you in Canandaigua and FLA. My family and I send our prayers. My kids always thought of your mom as their grandma. I am very honored to be one of your friends. Remember, we are one big family in the EMS field. Take care of yourself and be strong as I know you will.

Love always,
K. V. H.

May 28th, 2009

    Ken, there are very few people that you meet through your life that really make a difference. You are one of those people. You and Mickie, through training, guidance and friendship, helped me to accept and get through some pretty crazy times back in the mid-nineties. I think back on those times and truly believe that you may have helped in saving my life! I am truly thankful. I haven't really had too many heroes in my short thirty-eight years, but as a whole, you are one of the men that I truly believe is one of my heroes. After all that you have done and dedicated your life to, it seems kind of odd that you have to face such a challenge too. I think back to all those taxi runs I used to hate when I started to work for you and T. up there at FLA, but those rides made me dive into that job as a "medic" and give 100 percent. Though those experiences and all the emergencies with "Nauker", all of the time spent on the volley squad and all of the work we did in training—all make sense now. I have learned to handle what was ahead of me, how to deal with the hospitals, CA (cancer) treatments and the beginning of my mother's walk with the Lord. I also learned about MI's (myocardial infarctions) and the near death of my father that led to him just taking another path in life, we called a new beginning. Then under all of the pressure of nearly losing my marriage, newborn child, a family business, a career and maybe my life, to the stress of it all, I found a bottle of bourbon in my hand. I owe a lot of getting through all of that to you, Mickie and all those positive vibes that surrounded all of us that have been able to call you a friend. In these few words written from an old friend, I want you to know that you have always been in my prayers! I know for a fact that any man that can tell the story of "the night of the terrible tumble" and keep a straight face—this will only be a little hiccup in your life.

You take care and I will often raise a glass to one of the few true heroes that I have ever had the pleasure of calling *friend*. You will be fine! If there is anything that my family or I can do to help, you pick up that phone and call anytime of the day or night! Heck, you are as tough as nails anyway.

A. B.

May 29th, 2009

Ken, I will run the risk of sounding redundant because I feel a profound need to say these words: "You are an inspiration, Sir".

One of my biggest fears is, in fact, the greatest challenge which you are facing now. I have often wondered how I would react and what I would do. Now I have an inspiration, an example.

I watched my mother face a similar challenge in 1991 when I was just six years old. I didn't understand it then. Her fight was short and simple, yet it was still a fight, and she is still here, being the wind beneath my wings today.

I wish the same to you, Sir. In January of 2005, you became the wind beneath my "career wings". I can truly say that you have been nothing short of a father to me in the world of EMS. You have always believed in me, given me inspiration, pushed me to better myself and grow from my mistakes. You have given me opportunities to grow that I never would have had. If I develop into half the paramedic, half the leader, half the educator, heck, half the man you are, then I'll be all right.

As I am sitting here writing this tonight, it is my first night in my new house. I couldn't be happier in life and I owe quite a bit of that to you. I hope to have you and Mickie as our guests sometime soon.

As time goes on, I still continue to learn from you. Your challenge is teaching me more than I would have expected. First, you teach me strength. You are letting nothing keep you down and you still do the work of the people. Second, you teach love for family and friends. I am guilty of not spending enough time with either and I am changing that. Third, love of God. I consider myself to be a reverent man; however, I am going to work on becoming closer with our Savior and the Father. And last, but most certainly not least, is to Carpe Diem (Seize the day) and for that fact, to seize the moment. I will be putting that lesson to use in a little over a month. (It's a surprise, so I'll tell you after I do it.)

So mostly, in closing, Ken, I want you to know that you are in the thoughts and prayers of J. and myself. You truly are an amazing man, and I am honored to be a friend of yours and to work with and for you. Please don't give up and please don't loose that light in your eye.

God bless and enjoy life as you always have. Thank you for everything, and I will see you Monday morning.

J. H.

June 2nd, 2009

You were (and are) my inspiration to become a paramedic. I value all the time you took in class to teach us to practice Paramedicine the right way. Thank you for all the guidance along the way in class and at CES (Canandaigua Emergency Squad). My thoughts and prayers are with you and your family. Without sounding trite, get well soon!

J. L.

June 3rd, 2009

We are so happy that you received good news from the doctors. Keep fighting and we will keep praying! All our love and respect from our family.

J. B.

June 3rd, 2009

You rock! So good to hear of the encouraging news. Continued love and prayers.

R. T.

June 3rd, 2009

Ken, keep fighting. It's great to hear the news. We are thinking of you and Mickie every day.

J. L.

June 3rd, 2009

I am thinking of you and Mickie! I am happy to hear that the meds are helping you and you are able to again enjoy your bike.

We are always a phone call away and just a road over. If you need anything, we are there for you! We will continue to pray for you!

You are greatly loved and admired!

A. R.

June 3rd, 2009

Uncle Ken, I think about you every day and say a prayer for you every day. Keep up the fighting. You're doing a great job. I never doubted from day one that you were going to beat this. You are a strong person and have been an inspiration to *a lot* of people, myself included. I appreciate all that you have ever done for me (whether or not you realize you have done a lot for me), and I am there if you ever need anything in return—or just because!

Always know that we are always available anytime. As I've learned from personal experience, it's who you have around you and supporting you that allows you to keep the strength to do what needs to be done. If your strength ever starts to feel like it's withering, you have all of us (as seen from the testimonies written and, I'm sure, from many who have not yet written) to draw upon. Forgive me for speaking for many, but from what I've seen, they feel the same and are willing to give you whatever you require to overcome this challenge. Mickie, that goes for you too.

All our love,
A., R., A. and T. B.

June 3rd, 2009

Hey Boss, glad to hear the news. I am sure there will be more to follow. Have some great rides on your bike!

J. H.

June 4th, 2009

Hey Kenny, what great news! I see summer ahead of grabbing life and going for the joy.

Love you,
J. F. F.

June 4th, 2009

Hello Ken. S. and I are so happy you are feeling well enough to enjoy riding again. You are strong and you know you have a lot of people praying for you. So happy for you. This was a great idea to do and to keep your family and friends updated in private so we know how to keep praying for you.

Love,
T. and S. K.

June 4th, 2009

Ken, I will keep you in my thoughts and prayers. I'm glad to see that you are feeling better. You are a great man and have taught me so much in the eighteen months I have spent with you. Keep fighting.

T. S.

June 5th, 2009

Uncle Ken, I'm glad you are starting to feel better and that you are able to ride your bike again! We are here for you no matter what. Just let us know and we will be there. Whether to help around the house or just to talk! Thank you for being who you are and being there for me and my family anytime we needed you. You have touched so many lives in so many different ways. We all love you and are praying for you. With your strength and all the love of your family and friends, I know you can beat this! I love you and hope you know you can call me anytime!

Love,
S., L. C. and Kids

June 5th, 2009

Dear Ken, when I heard the news, I was saddened. But the next thought that immediately came to mind was, *Ken is one of the strongest persons I have ever known. He will beat this!* I remember visiting you in the hospital after your motorcycle accident and was amazed at how strong you were then. You had a big smile on your face when you were undoubtedly suffering. It really made me realize that we all should have that kind of strength. I know you are drawing on that strength right now. Your faith in God will guide you.

I never quite explained to you why I chose to give up EMS so soon after I finished my paramedic class. I would like you to know that you did inspire and guide me through it all. You were always there to listen to me when my fiery attitude surfaced. You probably were sitting there thinking, *Who is this crazy lady?* But you were calm and talked me through it and always had a solution no matter what the problem was. You know I drew from that and when faced with hairy situations out in the "field", I liked to think that I remained as calm.

It was a tough decision for me to leave EMS. It was in my blood and I certainly had the "bug". Maybe one day I will tell you why, but

I hope you were not too disappointed. If I could come back, I would in a second. I loved working for you and FLA. I had some of the best times of my life there. You were a pleasure to work for. I will be keeping you in my prayers. I know you are strong. If you need anything, please do not hesitate to call me or V.

"May God bless you and keep you all the days of your life". Thanks for being you! Everyone you have ever known has been touched by you somehow! Thank you and God bless.

K. Y.

June 11th, 2009

Uncle Ken, I was thinking of you at five thirty this morning while I was working. I felt that I should call, say hi and tell you that I loved you. When I got home, I saw your new journal entry and I knew why. God was letting me know that you needed some extra love and prayers.

As long as I can remember, you have always been a teacher. I know the decision to stop teaching was probably a really hard choice for you to make. I know that it is a passion you have, and you are great at it. In my eyes, your teaching has always reached far beyond the classroom. You have always been a role model for me. I admire, respect and look up to you. I also know there are many people who echo those sentiments.

Know that I love you and I am praying for you. I hope that you continue to stay ahead of the pain.

A. R.

June 11th, 2009

Hey Ken, the foundation you have built in the paramedic and other EMS programs is a strong one. I know you are going to miss it, but rest assured that there are *hundreds* of EMS providers who have benefited from your high-quality teaching skills. We are better prehospital-care providers because of you! *Also*, the impact you have had on current and future instructors has been superlative! You have always been my mentor as an EMS educator, even after having a student pass out on us when I was student teaching under your direction twelve years ago. No better way to teach "syncope" than to have someone actually do it! Cool!

Take care. We are all praying for you and you are correct—*God* does listen and will help you through the tough times! *That* I am sure of!

S. D.

June 11ᵗʰ, 2009

Good morning, Ken. I wanted to stop by and say hello and to let you know that you are in my thoughts and prayers. Please don't hesitate to contact me if you need anything at all.

It saddens me to see that you are ending your complete involvement with the paramedic program. Any of us who have taken the paramedic class have been touched and inspired in ways that future students will never understand. You are a true teacher, not just in name but also in practice. I am grateful and honored every time I practice, to know that you had a large hand in how I practice today.

Thank you for allowing us the opportunity to see what Paramedicine truly should be.

You will beat this. Anyone who knows you does not doubt that for one minute.

Thinking of you!

M. G.

June 11ᵗʰ, 2009

Dear Ken, it is truly the day that EMS in the Finger Lakes Region begins to blossom. You, as the skilled gardener, have taken it to this point; and it will grow because of all you have done.

EMS in the region, along with the residents, owe you a great debt of gratitude for which we can never repay. Your professionalism and dedication to the art of teaching has helped many students and, in turn, have saved countless lives.

God will help you and your family through this time, and you will beat the beast.

God bless you and yours, P. and K. H.

June 11ᵗʰ, 2009

Ken, I am so, so sorry to hear you are not going to be teaching. I know how much you love doing that. I never got the chance to attend any of your classes, but I've heard you are a wonderful teacher and the college has a wonderful, caring teacher. I know many people are going to be so sorry. We are still praying for you daily, and we are here for you any time.

Love,
T. and S. K.

June 12ᵗʰ, 2009

Ken, I am really sorry to hear that you will not being teaching the paramedic class anymore. You must concentrate on your health and your family. My prayers are with you. You have taught me a lot in the EMS field, both in class and outside of class, and I will always thank you for that. We have had a lot of old times together—bowling, riding together in Canandaigua, banquets...you name it. Keep up your spirits. We all love you! Take care and be safe.

K. V. H.

June 12ᵗʰ, 2009

You could never let your students down. You have made concessions to them over the years, and your students will make the same concession for you. The important thing is to put yourself first for a change.

J. D.

June 12th, 2009

Hi again, Kenny. I just want to let you know that I am so very touched by all the wonderful notes to you from people around you that have been able to connect through this amazing gift of the Caring Bridge. I'm sure they too are touched by all the love that surrounds you. Sweet dreams, sleep tight and may lots of healing energy come your way.

Love,
K.

PS I also finally found Pacific Time Zone. I don't know what time zone I was in before! Ha ha ha. Hey, I'm blond. What can I say?

Love,
K. L. H.

June 13th, 2009

Hi Kenny, I am really sorry to hear that the pain has returned with enough of a vengeance to make you have to leave doing something you love so much to do—teaching. Maybe those "fireside chats" and a good massaging recliner chair would help! The most important thing though is that you put yourself first. You deserve only the best. You have always given your best and I truly believe that God is a gentle and loving God and will help you on this new path. You are an amazing man and I send you tons of love and prayers. If there is anything I can do please let me know. Just so you know too, I have contacted many of my friends and have asked them to put you on their prayer lists at their churches, so many extra prayers are coming to you now too!

I am sooo happy that we had the opportunity to reconnect last weekend and visit at J. and B.'s home and to meet Mickie. She is a doll. Boy, oh, boy, she sure made a huge hit with T. and so did you! You look wonderful, strong and healthy. I'm praying that perfect health is returning to you each and every moment of each and every day. Thank you both for taking the time to make that visit happen. I only hope you weren't too uncomfortable in those metal chairs on the sun porch! Oy Vey! It really was a fun visit though, wasn't it? I hope when I come back home in August for a short visit, we will be able to do it again. Hey, have you had any rhubarb pie yet?

This growing-up business is definitely for the "birds" some-times. Change is not always what we want to do or easy in the first few steps, but usually, it works out for the best. You are, and always have been, an inspiration to me through your loving support of your family. Your strength as a man of honor is way before your years and through you being you. You are one of a very select special few angels of God and I know He is by your side walking this path with you. The rest of us whose lives you have touched are also there alongside you, sending strength and loving support to you all the way.

I am praying for your healing and return to good health. I thank you for sharing your lessons that you have been learning on your way too. Too often we just don't pay attention to our own "temple". We brush off the little warnings, the little alerts. It is time for you to take care of you, and don't even think about worrying about leaving your teachings at this point, as heartfelt and painful as it is. There will always be a place for your sharing your gifts with others.

Take good care, keep that beautiful smile and spirit going and savor every moment. I love you and am so happy to have you as part of my very special family. May God bless.

Your cousin, K. L. H.

June 13ᵗʰ, 2009

Hi Ken, had a pretty slow day on the fly car today. I've spent a good deal of my time thinking, reflecting, planning, dreaming and more. (Ahh, how the mind of a paramedic travels a million miles an hour like a duck.) I spent time looking at the past and thinking about the future.

The reason I am sharing this with you is that I found a constant in both my past and the thoughts of my future. That constant is your inspiration. As I, and so many others, have mentioned before, you inspired me in countless ways to get where I am today. In the thinking about where I am going, I found you as an inspiration again. As I strive to become an educator, and someday a manager, I will always think of you, your lesson, your work, your attitude and your ability to see the good in everything, no matter what it is.

But most importantly, I just want to share that I thought of you today and prayed for you. And in that prayer, I praised the Lord and gave Him thanks for having you in my life. You truly have been a blessing to me, and I will be forever grateful for that.

God bless you, Ken. Enjoy your Sunday and I will see you Monday morning.

J. H.

June 15ᵗʰ, 2009

I happened to be thinking about you and Mickie today and was wondering how you were doing, and your update popped up. God works in mysterious ways! Sorry to hear the pain is back, but stay strong as it is not easy, but you have a lot of prayers behind you.

J. B.

June 15ᵗʰ, 2009

Uncle Ken, my heart goes out to you. You've had to make a lot of tough decisions lately that I know have not been easy. Maybe making the decision to give up teaching full-time, for now, was God's way of showing you around this stumbling block and saying, "Hey, you've always given so much to others, now is the time to concentrate on you because if you are going to beat this 'beast' you need to concentrate on you".

In order to beat this, you need to be aware of what's going on in you, what is not right. Don't ignore the signs and please don't wait to call the doctor.

Faced with a similar situation years ago, I decided to give up college to fight my "beast". I knew I had to concentrate on the fight and return to my future later if I wanted to have a future later. Although I never returned to college on the path I thought I wanted to go, I ended up walking a path that provided me with a loving family (in addition to the one I already had). Also, a job that provided me with the angels and support I needed to get me through another really tough time. They kept my job open for me and wouldn't let me quit because I had proved myself, and they had faith I (we) would overcome the situation at hand, and they were right. She's graduating!

I believe you also have your angels through all you have done with the paramedic program and beyond. I believe you will have the opportunity to teach again and live without the pain you are currently experiencing. I believe you are strong. Have the faith, have the fight and the will to overcome this. You have many that support you, love you and stand behind you in this battle.

If you get a chance, listen to a song by Trisha Yearwood, "You Don't Have to Move That Mountain". I think of you every time I listen to and pray that God will show you the way around each stumbling block you have to encounter.

I think of you every day and pray for you every day. We are always available to stand behind you in your battle or beside you if you need.

All my love,
A. B.

June 15th, 2009

Hi Kenny, I'm sorry to hear today's news. I am saying prayers for you constantly and will continue to do so. You are strong and as your niece said, you have lots of angels around you. God and the universe do work in strange ways, but I agree, it's time for you to take care of you. Don't be afraid to call the doctors and please don't ignore things. We are all by your side in our thoughts and prayers. We will help hold you up and you walk strong.

Life is too short and too precious. Learning that gift is something the whole world would be better off knowing, instead of wasting time being unhappy, arguing, hating, etc.

Hang in there, kiddo. Lots and lots of love and prayers.

K. L. H.

June 15th, 2009

Hi Kenny. The song recommendation is also done by Allison Krause, and it's a great song to keep your spirits high. It's one of my favorites. I am sorry that your pain has gotten so aggressive. I agree, don't wait. I am sending you a big hug. You are the best.

Lots of love,
J. F. F.

June 15th, 2009

Ken, I pray that your pain will be eased and that you are able to sleep tonight under the watchful eyes of your angels. I hope that you find this prayer comforting.

"May God ease your pain, increase your faith and decrease your fears. May God continue to give you strength—body, mind and soul. May blessings, love and joy surround you. Amen."

S. D.

June 16th, 2009

Ken, I know words can't take the pain away, but may all the prayers and encouraging messages ease your heart to know how much you are cared for. We are all there for you wherever, whenever and however!

God bless,
T. K.

June 16th, 2009

Good morning, Ken. I never thought I would be looking for words to say to you, so I am not even going to try! I just want you to know that you and Mickie are in our thoughts and prayers. Your angels are watching over you and God is walking beside you each step of the way.

L. C.

June 16th, 2009

See, sunshine and friends are the best medicine for anyone. Maybe we need solar-powered ambulances so that the sun can shine in on the patients. What do you think? Keep up the smiles and the good spirits. Together as a family, we will all help you beat this.

Love,
The J.B. Family

June 16th, 2009

Ken, what more can I say that has not already been said? It is nice to see that everyone you have touched in your life feels the same way and I fall in the same category. You scared the heck out of me all the time while working at FLA. Then I decided to go to the paramedic class, and you still scared the heck out of me at work and at class. Until the day "I had to ride with you" in the fly car, and I saw the true Mr. Kelly. A great Paramedic, a great man and a true inspiration. So in closing, I now live in Texas with my family and am doing great. Also, if you think at any point you are going to leave us, you better give one heck of a notice.

With love,
M. K., your son! (LOL)

June 16ᵗʰ, 2009

Ken, it sounds like a tougher than usual week. Nothing like a little sunshine and fresh air to make you feel better though. It's amazing how such simple things make such a difference.

As always you know I'm available to help with whatever is needed.

B. C.

June 16ᵗʰ, 2009

Ken, it seems that what works for me is the old-fashioned chat, one-on-one with God like you are doing. I don't have the same problem as you, but to each his or her problem is monumental. I've gone through the drowning of my eight-year-old daughter, the death of two brothers one year after the other (they were in their late thirties), totally by surprise. The suicide of my sister-in-law a year after my last brother's death and now my father's hospitalization. Whew! I didn't realize how this all sounded until I wrote it out! If it wasn't for my faith in God and in the promises of the Bible, I would be a total mess. He has the plan. He has and is the Way, the Truth and the Life. We need to get onboard with His plan instead of expecting Him to get on our plans. So chin up, squash down the dragon of cancer and march on forward. Proud that you are on God's track!

God bless,
D. T.

June 16th, 2009

Hi Kenny! I'm glad to hear you are doing better today. You know it's okay to not feel perfect or not be perfect all the time. My stepdad used to say, "Nobody's perfect—that's why they put erasers on pencils". That's been one of my favorite sayings!

You are strong and loved by so many. I'm excited that all our loving energy and prayers are helping to lift you up. I've been thinking about you and saying extra prayers for your healing and for healing of everyone that I love and care about.

It is an amazing feeling when you are hurting and not feeling good to wake up in the morning and realize God has given you a new day with the sunshine, the birds, the flowers, the blue sky and the fresh air. There is no lack of abundance in the universe with prayer and good wishes surrounding you. Keep smiling, keep the powerful faith you have and keep sharing your feelings. That is healing for everyone you share them with, a reminder to us all that life is good. Life is short, and wasting energy by being angry, being unhappy or being depressed is not what it is all about. Thanks for the wake-up call reminders. Have a beautiful day!

I am also so glad that we all have this wonderful avenue through Caring Bridge to stay in touch.

K. L. H.

June 16th, 2009

Hey Ken, I was so happy I had that time with you on your porch. It convinced me that the fight is still in you. Rumors from others usually do prove to be false! I love when I hear you speak

29

of your relationship with God. It inspires me. Actually, you have always inspired me to be a better supervisor and paramedic but, most importantly, a person. I have not always been that, but knowing you and watching your fight has and will continue to inspire me in my walk with the Lord and life. God bless and continue the good fight. He is with you.

K. G.

June 16ᵗʰ, 2009

I follow your journey through this great vehicle. So you were a little down in the dumps. There is no shame in that. You do not need to be strong all the time, that is what your lovely wife and friends are for. We are here to help keep you on the right path. Of course, with God's help anything is possible.

You need to enjoy each and every day and remember that even out of the dark rain and dismal days, a gorgeous rose is made.

P. and K.H.

June 17ᵗʰ, 2009

Ken, you never feel you should have to tell everyone you are sorry for expressing how you feel. That is what this site is all about. It is for you, not us. We are just here to see you through. We all care. That is why we worry, and we will, even if you don't write what really is on your heart. At least when you write the truth, we know how to pray for you and Mickie. This is the best place to express yourself, so please continue so we can help walk you through. Please read Psalm 103. I think it is a very encouraging Psalm.

God bless,
T. K.

June 18ᵗʰ, 2009

Just stopping in to give love and prayers. Stay strong and hope to see you soon.

J. B.

June 18ᵗʰ, 2009

Hi Kenny. I'm so sorry that the cancer keeps aggressing on you so much. You mentioned a beautiful song ("I Have a Dream"), and the words are really touching.

I remember my prayers to God when I thought I was dying a few years ago (the chest pains and breathing, I thought I was having a heart attack plus I felt like you know what). I kept thinking, *I'm not ready yet, God. There is still so much I have to accomplish. I'm not afraid, but I'm not ready.*

I can understand some of the feelings you are experiencing. I guess the best thing is to stay in the present and live each moment to your fullest. Mentally send the pain and cancer away and surround yourself with a thick wall of the white light of God and your angel guide's protection. Everyone that we miss and love that are up in Heaven now, I'm sure, are surrounding you with love and protection. Everyone here who loves and cares about you is doing the same. My sister J. is one of those special angels too. Her thoughtfulness, generosity and love are amazing. I hope the chair helps to relieve your discomfort and you have fun doing your "fireside chats" to your students. Hey, you could even do it from home with some electronics.

I love you and am praying for you right now. Hang in there and give my love to Mickie too. She is also one of your angels here on earth. I'm sending love and prayers for healing to you both.

K. L. H.

June 18th, 2009

Hi again from Ms. Verbose! There was another song that came out a few years ago. I think it was a Country and Western song. The author and singer had been diagnosed with cancer also. It was about the wake-up call he got and what he decided to do about it rather than "waiting to get around to it". We all know about "round tuits". They usually don't happen. It had words something like, "I went sky diving, horseback riding, rocky mountain climbing, I rode a bull in three point two". I can't remember the name of the song or the singer, but it was a great and touching song. It was about realizing time is short, so do your "dreams" now. I'm sure someone out there remembers that tune. Its words are powerful too, not only if you are sick but you are healthy too. It's about realizing time is precious and short for all of us and can be snapped away in a heartbeat. It's something that I know you especially, and all of your paramedic friends and students, are aware of daily just because of the precious field of work you have devoted yourselves to. I'm sure all of those people who you all have helped are surrounding you with love and support too. Lots and lots of angels surround you all, as it takes a very special kind of person to do the work you do.

Remember that nobody has ever laid on their death bed and said, "Gee, I wish I had gone and done more work today".

Have a beautiful day and smell the fresh air and the flowers!

Love from chatty K. L. H.

June 18th, 2009

Hi! The song that K. is referring to is by Tim McGraw called "Live Like You Were Dying". It is a good song that does remind everyone to take each day and live life it to the fullest.

As long as I can remember, I have always liked the scripture Ecclesiastes 3:1–8, "*There is a time for everything*". At times when I thought I wanted to give up, it reminded me that in every situation, especially those hard ones, good will come of it in some way. Even though it may not be cut and dried or easy to identify. The other is 1 Corinthians 13:4–13. I am a strong believer in the power of love, loving and being loved.

We are continuing to pray for you. Always know that you are loved and you will not walk this alone.

A. R.

June 18th, 2009

Ken, Monday I signed this guest book and prayed that you would have a peaceful and restful night of sleep. Tuesday, you made a journal entry that you had just that! The power of prayer is truly remarkable and powerful. It's the little things like that that continue to increase my faith and the power of God.

When I tell people that I am the Chaplain of the Oaks Corners Fire Department, first they laugh and, with the language I use, I don't blame them. Then I tell them how proud I am of my service toward my brother and sister firefighters and EMS's and their families. I never want to be a fire chief—I *always* want to be a fire Chaplain! My faith in God is strong, and I am humbled by yours! Don't loose that faith as more difficult days may be ahead. Know that your many friends are here for you and will always be!

Ride on, brother, and let me know when you want to go for a ride! My rice burner needs to be aired out a bit! It's getting dusty in the garage!

May the Lord bless you and keep you strong!

S. D.

June 18th, 2009

Hi Ken! It's days like today that make me want to scream! Thank you for jumping in to save me today. It's always good to know you have an ear on everything and you always know when it's hitting the fan. The best part about today was being able to laugh through it. You always make the job seem easier even when I am ready to pull out my hair. I just wanted to say thanks for everything you do. We all stand beside you and the angels watch over you.

L. C.

June 18ᵗʰ, 2009

Ken, I've known you for over thirty-five years and you have never been alone. You have always had friends and family who respect and love you. It is like life itself: we just have blinders on and don't see clear at times. You have spent your whole life wanting to take care of your family. It is now time for you to take care of yourself and Mickie. You need to enjoy life, your family and your friends. I know I've told you this many times—we love you!

T. K.

June 18ᵗʰ, 2009

Uncle Ken, I was so encouraged to hear you had a restful sleep and a beautiful day on Tuesday. Thank you for listening to your body and calling the doctor, but I'm sorry the news is not what you expected. From your last message, it seems that you are at peace with the *possible* outcome, where at the beginning, your worst fear was leaving those behind (as is anybody who received the dreaded cancer diagnosis). Now that you have accepted the outcome and you seem to be at peace with the leaving issue, you can really concentrate on what needs to be done to move on. Everything about this diagnosis is a step-process, a progression, that we all go through who have received this kind of news. I cannot even begin to tell you how many dreams and scenarios I came up with to tell my family I was not going to make it to a ripe old age!

Please don't "feel bad" or hold back what you are feeling because of the "worry" you might cause any of us. We are here for you, no matter what. As testimony from your previous entry, the response, prayers and encouragement you were sent that allowed you to be at peace in your mind and that allowed you that restful sleep. Sometimes, knowing you are not alone in this battle is all it takes to take the next step or give you the strength to go on. As the oldest child, we tend to feel we need to have to be strong for everybody else. What we tend to forget is that the strength we portrayed over the years has sunk in. We need to allow those that we were strong for to be able to repay that strength and prove that the lesson taught was well learned. I for one have learned your lesson well.

Music has always been a huge part of my life and gotten me through some times. The reason being is that I always thought that if the song pertained to me and my situation, it pertained to whoever wrote that song. It touched whoever sang that song and the countless others who bought that song, which led me to believe that I was never alone. There are many talented writers out there and the one who came up with the phrase, "*And I've come far enough to know that love's worth never letting go, and love is not a matter of pride*", was truly on target. We love you, thick or thin, good or bad, in sickness and in health—no holds barred!

I have a good friend whose sister was diagnosed with stage four breast cancer and was given six months to live. She lived more than six years beyond her projected prognosis, and her doctors were amazed at her strength and will to live. We believe the main reason she succumbed to the disease is because her immediate family (husband and kids) gave up the fight and so did she. I want you to know, *we will never give up on you*, as long as you are willing to fight. Even if you are not, we will be fighting for you!

I hope you had a wonderful class in a comfortable chair and a worthy "fireside chat" tonight. You deserve it.

Love,
A. B.

June 21ˢᵗ, 2009

Hi Uncle Ken. I want you to know that I agree with every-thing mom said in the post before me. LOL. She certainly has a way with words, how to express verbally what other people feel. I know that my mother would not be who she is today without you and I also know that I wouldn't be who I am today without her. So thank you. Thank you for being such a strong, positive influence on those around you. You have made such a significant impact on our family and I am truly honored to call you my uncle. Know that there are a lot of people in a lot of places thinking of you and praying for you, myself included. I look forward to seeing you the next time I am home.

Love always,
A. B.

June 22ⁿᵈ, 2009

Ken and Mickie, our thoughts and prayers are with you both and let us know if either of you need any help with anything. Ken, you can always count on P.'s "cheery" personality to brighten your day!

Seriously, we are thinking of you and are here if you need anything.

P. and S. G.

June 23ʳᵈ, 2009

Hi Kenny and Mickie. I just wanted to say hi and send you lots of love and blessings tonight. It is about ten thirty, California time. I've been thinking about you and want to say, "Thanks, Mickie, for the nice, sweet note I received from you today". I then looked at some of the pictures from our Sunday night dinner a week ago and just got lots of "warm huggies" from the pictures. I think they were the pictures you sent to J. or vice versa.

Kenny, I love you and am sending lots of love and healing prayers your way. May you always be as strong, healthy and beautiful as you look in those pictures. Mickie, you, my dear sweet new cousin (that Aunt G. was crazy about and told me so), I'm so glad we had that time together and finally met in person! I am sending lots of love, blessings and healing too. I look forward to seeing you both again when I'm home in August. Mickie, do you know how special you are? Do you know that cute little three-year-old we are all crazy about, T. F. Man, oh, man, he sure picked you two out as very, very special people. That in itself is a special touch from God and the angels.

May you both have a beautiful and wonderful week and lots of love, prayers and healing energy coming your way. Kenny, as Aunt S. used to say to me, "We're all family and that's the most important thing and we're stuck together just like Kodak glue"! I haven't gotten ahold of B.A. yet. I sent an email and it got returned, but I will call him this week. He is a very, very strong, loving support to our family. He is one of those angels and so is his wife A. I promise to call them tomorrow.

Aunt S. was right, we need to stay in touch and in love. We need to know and be aware that life is short and can be snapped away in a heartbeat. Family comes first. We grew up across the street from Aunt S. and Uncle J. A. and they were one of the best gifts we had in our childhood.

Time to go get beauty sleep. I need all the beauty sleep I can get, ha ha ha. Sweet dreams and know you are surrounded by love and prayers.

Lots of love,
K. L. H.

June 23rd, 2009

Ken, our family is praying for you and Mickie. Thanks for being such a good teacher, boss and all-around good guy. If you need anything, please let us know.

S. P. and Family

June 25th, 2009

Ken, just a note to say hello. I woke in the middle of the night last night and felt I needed to pray for you. I hope you are getting some sleep at night. Enjoy today and do try to rest a little during the day. Maybe the staff at Finger Lakes can get a nice lounge cot for you there too so you can rest during down time. Sending you our prayers and love.

S. and T. K.

June 25th, 2009

Happy Thursday! Just letting you know you are still in our thoughts and prayers.

J. B.

June 26th, 2009

Ken, I was just outside walking the tracks and I noticed you out there watching the weather. As I watched you, I wondered what was going through your mind. Were you actually thinking, *I'm going to ride my bike in the rain*, or were you looking to the sky for guidance?

As I read how you talk to God, I giggle because you often refer to yourself as God. I realize there are a few similarities: you both have a heart of gold, you oversee what others see as themselves as failures and you have voices that rumble the wind but say things that calm the storm.

I'm sure God and His angels will guide you through this rough ride. I mean, you are best friends, right? Thinking of you!

S. R.

June 27ᵗʰ, 2009

Mr. Kelly, I just found out the news. I want you to know that you and Mickie are in my thoughts and prayers every day. I want to thank you for being there for me through all of my trying times. I miss so much seeing you and having you smile and saying good morning every day at FLA. You treated me not only like an employee, but like a father. I knew I could always talk to you about anything. Thank you so much also for being there for me at the hospital. You and Mickie mean so much to me and my family. I miss you and wish you the best of luck with everything. My thoughts and prayers are with you.

D. P.

June 28ᵗʰ, 2009

Hi Kenny. Thinking of you both.

Love,
J. F. F.

June 29ᵗʰ, 2009

Ken, I have told you this before but feel compelled to write it again. There are times in your life where situations and people will shape the future. Sometimes we believe it to be circumstance, but truly there is a plan for all things. Right now, this is the biggest challenge in your life, and true to form, you are handling things with dignity and concern for those around you. You were one of those people who shaped my future, and I forever value the lessons, support and direction you provided for me and my family. I know that you have made a difference in the lives of many people and will continue to do so. God has His arms around you no matter what comes or happens. Know that K., J., T., and I are thinking of you and praying for you and Mickie. Hope to see you soon.

M. T.

July 1st, 2009

Ken, I want to say thank you. Even when I had no hope in myself, you found it in me and guided me through the paramedic class. Without you telling me I can do this, I would have never finished the class. I know that I was never your model employee, but I always looked up to you and thought, *I will never be as good as him.* Ken, you are like a father figure to me even though I do not work for you anymore. I will always consider myself a part of the FLA family.

Good luck,
J., A. and N. P.

July 2nd, 2009

Ken, just letting you know that I am thinking of you and Mickie. I truly know you will fight this head on, not only because of your strength but everyone else's piled on too. You have to be the smartest and best paramedic I have known and worked with. I know I try and teach my classes as you do—teaching with the highest of standards and knowledge—but know I will never compare with the Master!

C. F.

July 3rd, 2009

I am saying prayers for you each day. I am hoping for good news so that you can also collect your "welfare" payments called Social Security. The sun has just come out, so go out and enjoy yourself this weekend.

J. D.

July 7th, 2009

Hi Kenny, I hope you are feeling better and that good news from the doctors comes your way. You truly are surrounded by angels. Why does it take something like this illness for us all to stop, smell the roses and go back to what really is important—love, support, family and friends? Our world has just gotten too fast, too "not caring" and too busy to slow down and simplify until something hits us like your illness.

I am sorry you are going through this and saddened about it too especially since you and Mickie have finally found each other and have time for you both. You have always taken care of others from when you were a little kid. I guess God picked the one who He knew was strongest to have to go through the "challenges" you've been going through in your life so that you can help teach the others around you more about life and love.

We all are learning from you in so many ways. You are still teaching us new things every day just by your strength and being *you*! I pray for both of you and send lots of love and healing energy as do all the amazing friends and angels around you. All I can say is *wow*, what an amazing support and strength you have and you have around you. Keep that white light all around you both. I am glad that the chair that J. has sent you is helping—she is one of your angels too.

Love,
K. L. H.

July 8ᵗʰ, 2009

Ken, I read your post today and was saddened that you are suffering and in pain. K. and I have just gone through this terrible ordeal and I can imagine what you are going through.

God and your friends will help you through this rough patch, just keep the faith.

P. H.

July 8ᵗʰ, 2009

My dear Ken, I am not real sure that what is written here will make any difference; yet I am compelled to reach out, to hold you, to let you know that there are many that respect, appreciate and love you. We all will make this journey at some point; and I, for one, pray that I will have your strength, resolve and faith. Yes, Jesus will be there when you arrive. The angels are walking with you now, some in human form, I feel. You will see the face of God, and there are many mortals that are here to lift you up and carry you if we must, as you travel this road. You and Mickie are continually in our prayers. God bless and keep you! We love you!

R. T.

July 8ᵗʰ, 2009

You are in our prayers. Fight until you can't fight any more, and then God will fight for you. Keep up your strength and live life to the fullest.

The B. Family

July 8ᵗʰ, 2009

Hello friend, I want to send you all of my positive thoughts and prayers. I am here for you no matter the time of day or the place. You fight this fight with an entire brigade of loving family and friends. XOXOXOXOXOXOXOXOXOXO.

L. Y.

July 8ᵗʰ, 2009

I hadn't noticed any trouble today from the outside except that you came in late. Your ability to press on in your many roles in spite of your own challenges is an inspiration and gives others strength and hope.

B. C.

July 9ᵗʰ, 2009

Ken, I am so sorry to hear you had a bad night again. I know no one can know what you are going through, but people have gone through it. Do you know you are loved and there are many, many people praying for you? We don't understand why, but we know God does. He is your strength and comforter. Psalm 119:50, *"My comfort in my suffering is this; Your promise preserves my life"*. We are here for you anytime. God bless.

T. and S. K.

July 9ᵗʰ, 2009

Hi Mr. Kelly. It's C. D., A.'s other half. I just wanted to let you know that you are in our thoughts, and we are sending all our positive energy your way. Again, I offer you Reiki. Either from us, or we can refer you to someone if that makes you more comfortable. It can help with the pain as well as healing. Any ammo to fight the beast, you know! You have an army behind you!

A. K.

July 10th, 2009

Uncle Ken, I am so glad to hear that your tests came back clear! This is awesome. We are all still praying for you and thinking about you daily. We are here for you anytime you need us. I love you!

Love,
L. C.

July 10th, 2009

I am so glad that the tests came back negative. Keep the faith and God will keep fighting with you.

L. R. T.

July 11th, 2009

Dearest Uncle Ken, what wonderful news! We have been praying for you and God does answer prayers! We will continue to pray for you and support you in any way you need. You are a strong man and have many people who love you.

Love,
A. R.

July 11th, 2009

Ken, praise the Lord! We are so excited for you and also for Mickie. We are going to continue to pray for you every day.

Love,
T. and S. K.

July 12th, 2009

Ken, your news is great! I don't think there is a day that I don't think of you and Mickie. You are both in our prayers. Thanks for the update.

L. C.

July 12th, 2009

Uncle Ken, *awesome*! So glad to hear of the recent news. This kind of news seems to renew your own personal faith and strengthen the resolve of the fight. It lets you know that you are winning, one battle at a time. Eventually, all these little battles will result in the victory you so well deserve.

Keep your faith, and know that if your personal faith is dwindling, there is an abundance, a tremendous surplus if you will, of faith and hope that is at your disposal, any time you need some extra to supplement your own. Also know this supply will never run out, so take as much as you need and some extra. Mickie, there's plenty there for you too to use as you need. I hope you take advantage of that.

I think about you both every day. Thanks to all of your angels and to God for providing them for you, to guide and support you through this challenge.

All our love,
A. and R. B.

July 12th, 2009

Ken, you are in our thoughts and prayers. Not a day goes by that you and Mickie do not cross our minds. If you need *anything* do not hesitate to ask.

K. L.

July 13th, 2009

Yeah, good news. We'll keep praying. You stay strong.

Love from us all,
J. B.

July 14th, 2009

Ken, I find myself fighting back the tears to even be writing on this page. You are my hero and my idol. If I can only pass along half of what you have taught and shown me, I will be lucky. I am so glad you enjoyed the book as it started me on the road to becoming a Tigger and no longer an Eeyore! You are in my prayers nightly. I will tell you the same thing I told my mother in her dark days. All you need to do is call or text me, and I will be there in a moment's notice. I will carry you for however long you may need me to. God made my shoulders capable of great things and your weight will be no burden on them but a blessing. My legs can go for miles, and I will fear nothing for the strength you have taught me will prevail over anything that may be placed in our path. You just let me know when the time is right and hold on so you can see what you created and finally reap the benefits! You are truly a second father to me and I can say that I am who I am because of you. Thank you.

C. D.

July 16th, 2009

Good morning! I hope you had an easy night, with the beast being caged. Really, I just wanted to let you know I am thinking of you and you are always in my family and my prayers.

C. C.

July 17th, 2009

Hey Ken, it's so awesome to see you're feeling good. I thought that was the case. I was glad I had the opportunity to get the pups over to you this week. Anything to cause a smile is definitely a good thing and works just as well as prayers. Keep fighting and enjoying life, Sir. It's working! If you need anything, you know where I am.

God bless,
J. H.

July 17th, 2009

Ken, I was reading the entries in your guestbook. A lot of people love you. You have made a big impression on them as you did for me. My prayers are with you and Mickie. My family and I love you, and we want you to be around for a long time.

Love,
K. H.

July 17th, 2009

I am glad that you put these encouraging updates on for us to read. It shows that prayer, care, love and concern work!

Thank you,
D. T.

July 17ᵗʰ, 2009

It was wonderful to hear that you had a good week! We continue to pray for you.

A. R.

July 17ᵗʰ, 2009

Ken, we are so happy to hear the beast has been in its cage this week. We will continue to pray that it stays there and that you continue to have good weeks. We pray that you will have many, many more peaceful and pain free nights of sleeping. We are sending you our love and prayers.

God bless,
T. and S. K.

July 17ᵗʰ, 2009

To have you laugh and joke with us is a wonderful gift. It's nice to have you come into the office and chat. I know it makes my day in the "cage" a little easier. It's true that there are times when I wanted to run from FLA, but the "family" kept me here. Minus the year and a half I was out for my back, the last eleven years have helped me grow as a person. There is not one person that I know that doesn't look up to you and cherish having you as a part of their life. Through the years, you and Mickie have supported many of us in some way and there is no way to say thank you. You both mean the world to me as well as so many others. Thank you for everything you do.

L. C.

July 17ᵗʰ, 2009

Uncle Ken, so happy to hear you had a good week without the pain and with plenty of rest. This kind of news really makes you appreciate the phrase "stop and smell the roses". You have yet again been an inspiration!

We love you,
R. and A. B.

July 17ᵗʰ, 2009

Dear Ken, it is great to hear that the beast is in its cage now. I am very happy to hear that you are getting your rest now too. If you or Mickie need anything, and I mean anything, please don't hesitate to call K. or myself. If this means at two in the morning if you want ice cream, please call! I have done that run many times in my tenure at FLA.

Please take care, my friend and until we talk again, know you and your whole family and friends are in my and K.'s prayers. God bless and keep you safe.

P. H.

July 18ᵗʰ, 2009

So glad to hear that you are feeling better and getting some rest! Enjoy this beautiful weather we are having—*finally*!

S. D.

July 21ˢᵗ, 2009

Hi Kenny, glad you are still ahead of the game. I talked with L. yesterday and caught her up on your situation. Naturally, she is very sad and sends you all of her love and a hug. She has no computer, so K. and I keep her informed. Lots of Kannenberg stubbornness is backing you up, Cuz.

Love you,
J. F. F.

July 23rd, 2009

We are praying for you.

S. P.

July 27th, 2009

Keep up your strength, and we will keep on praying.

J. B.

July 30th, 2009

Ken, you are continually in our prayers. Seize the day, Boss! Miracles happen! God is great, beer and cookies are good, and you know people are crazy!

Our love always,
R. and S. T.

July 30th, 2009

Hi Kenny, sorry I haven't written. I hope you are staying strong and feeling better today. Hang in there, Kiddo. Lots of love and prayers coming your way. I'll be home in Rochester from the thirteenth to the twenty-fourth of August. Hope to see you and Mickie during that time. Lots of love and keep on being strong. Keep on being the incredible man you are and always have been.

Love,
K. L. H.

August 2nd, 2009

Hello Uncle Ken. Sorry I haven't been in touch, but I am keeping updated with how you are doing. You are in my thoughts and prayers every day. I hope to be able to come and visit you sometime in the near future. School has been keeping me busy. I love you.

S. K.

August 4th, 2009

That's awesome news, Ken!

S. D.

August 4th, 2009

Hooray for you!

Love,
J. F. F.

August 4th, 2009

Mr. Kelly, raise a cookie and say, "Ha, you damn beast"!

Always in our prayers,
B. C. and D. R.

August 4ᵗʰ, 2009

Ken, such *great* news and so pleased to hear it. *Miracles* happen—believe!

R. T.

August 4ᵗʰ, 2009

This is wonderful news! We will continue to pray and be there for you. The kids had a blast yesterday visiting you. That was all they talked about afterward! Enjoy the summer weather this week. Excellent bike weather, I hear!

Love,
A. R.

August 4ᵗʰ, 2009

God bless, that's awesome news!

K. G.

August 11ᵗʰ, 2009

You and Mickie continue to be in our prayers. May you be blessed with His grace and healing.

Love to you both,
S. and R. T.

August 11ᵗʰ, 2009

Hi Kenny! Sounds like from your last entry that things are going along okay. I sure hope so! I know you have so much love, prayers and support coming your way. You are an amazing man and don't deserve this huge "challenge" in your life, but God and the universe work in funny ways. Your challenge is teaching humility, strength, love and support to the rest of us who love and care about. Thank *you* for being *you*. You are walking in strong, happy footsteps of Aunt G. and you're making us all prouder than we've ever been. Please keep the love and positive outlook always in your heart. I know what Aunt G. would be saying, smiling and passing on the love too.

I'm leaving early tomorrow morning for New York and will arrive late in the evening. Right now I'm procrastinating about packing! I hope to see you at J. and B.'s thirty-fifth anniversary party on the twenty-second, and the rest of the family that will be there too. Keep well and know you are loved and respected oh sooo much.

Love,
Your Cuz, K. L. H.

August 11ᵗʰ, 2009

Hi Kenny, I just talked with L. H. She is without a computer. If you want her phone number, I have it in my cell. She sends lots of love, prayers, and best wishes to you from herself and her family in Missouri.

PS How in the heck did we all so suddenly get older? Kids, enjoy and savor your journey. It passes quickly.

Love to all,
K. L. H.

August 12ᵗʰ, 2009

Hello Ken, just a note to say we are still standing with you in spirit and praying continually for you.

T. and S. K.

August 13th, 2009

God has blessed us with someone like you. You feel free to cry, weep, scream, or anything else. You have, and will have, always my love, support and admiration.

God bless you.

K. G.

August 13th, 2009

Mr. Kelly, I too referred to Job while going through the loss of my daughter, as he lost his children too. The records of Jobs trials suggests that he too suffered. May I suggest that he was not "tearless". I am sure that he too may have cried at his loss and all that he went through. He just did not have a shower to be alone in. I also want to remind you of Moses. A mighty leader of the Israelites, who led them through the great battles with the Amalekites, battling day and night with the Israelites winning, while his staff was raised. When he got tired, as all of us would have with a day and night battle, his arms grew weak; and he would lower them, causing the Israelites to loose and die in battle. When he got his second, fifteenth, and one hundredth wind and raised the staff, they would become victorious. Now imagine the anguish he too went through. The fatigue, the pain and the heartbreak knowing that some were lost because of his "weakness". He too didn't have a shower; but he had those who came alongside him, raised his arms and held them upright until the Israelites were the total victors! You too, Mr. Kelly, have those who come alongside and raise your arms for you. We think of you, pray for you, assist you, and make sure at work we don't give you a reason to "red chair us". We will raise your arms when you grow weary. You have your own Aarons and Joshuas allowing you to fight this battle for your life—and we are honored!

D. T.

August 13ᵗʰ, 2009

Oh, my dear Kenny, it is not weak or selfish to have fears, grief, feelings of being overwhelmed and pain. It is not weak to cry at any time and to cry on your own behalf as part of the healing process. My dear cousin, I have been witness to many of the past losses you have experienced in your life and I was there for many of them. You have always quietly and strongly stood, letting others lean on you, asking nothing in return.

It is a measure of how much you love that you are weeping for future losses. But remember, we only have this moment. The past is a cancelled check and the future is unwritten. All we have is this moment; and at this moment, you are blessed, even though you hurt.

The God I know does not ask us to be stoic or to judge our own pain. My God asks only that you love and that you remember that you aren't alone. Learning to receive is part of that and learning to love ourselves is even a bigger part. Crying for our losses, for our shattered dreams and for our pain are part of learning that we too are children of that Greatness. If we never have need, how can we ever really understand that part of the love? How can we understand that unconditional means—all of it? In the end, all of it is good and our needs too will be met. Perhaps not as we think they should be or as we want them, but we are loved without any reservation, and they will be met, no matter what.

I am sorry for your pain, deeply sorry that you are suffering. I am joyful for the blessing of relief you have received from your friends at the college. I am happy for the expression of the respect that you are held in that they will bring in the best minds. I am not surprised that it will take a full crew to do what you have done by yourself. You have given a great gift of service, and it's now your turn to receive caring. It's all part of the wheel of life.

It's so hard to be vulnerable when you have been strong, but it's not a failure. It is the just opposite; it is a gateway for a new kind of strength.

I love you and am sending you a big hug.

J. F. F.

55

August 13ᵗʰ, 2009

Ken, after reading J.'s and D.'s notes to you, it is difficult to find the words and to set emotions aside. I cried as well as I read your entry. I prayed that God would give us who love and care for you so deeply your pain, each a little bit, to lessen your burden. Please do not be ashamed of your own tears! I remember vividly watching the *Passion of Christ*. In the last scene, a single tear fell from the sky. To me it was the tear of our God, crying at the loss of Christ, His son, our Savior. Surely, if God can cry, you can as well. Be not ashamed!

S. and I, your family, the people around you, the staff at the college and at FLA are here to hold you, to love you, to care for you and to care about you.

God bless and keep you!

S. and R. T.

August 13ᵗʰ, 2009

Ken, our hearts cry out to God for you each day. In your strong silence, when you are out and about, we, who know you and love you, know you are hurting. I know if any one of us could, we would take the pain from you we would. You have always been so strong and held in your hurts and pains for many years, not letting anyone know that you were hurting. Now is the time for you to receive the love that family, friends and coworkers want to share with you. There are many, many people who love you, care for you and are praying for you hourly. Do not be sorry for telling us how you are each time you write. This is a safe place for you, just like the shower, only we get to send you messages to help you. It helps us to pray for you. You are with us every day and many times in the middle of the night.

Love,
S. and T. K.

August 13th, 2009

Uncle Ken, I wish you wouldn't feel sorry for crying. Crying is one way our bodies relieve stress (even though it is said to be a "female" trait). We all need to relieve stress in some way. Crying just reminds us that we are human and still alive because we still have feelings. Crying for all the things you might miss is not being selfish because all the things and events you want to participate in, the other participants want you there too. So in my eyes, that is no way selfish. That just enforces how much you care about others. Also, how much you know they care about you. So in the future, if you feel you need to cry, do so, even if it is in the private space of the shower.

I wish I could carry some of your burdens for you and know that I can't. However, I will be available any time to hold your arms up (as Moses in the story) to help and aid you to win this battle.

Mom sent me an email, which immediately reminded me of your battle against this beast, so I have forwarded it to you. You have been so strong throughout this process and carried the load you've been given without asking for any relief. The message, as I determined it, is that God only gives us what we can handle. Each test is a building block to empower us with the perseverance and the tools to cross the chasm, whatever and whenever it may be.

Know that you have an *army* of troops behind you to do whatever is needed to win and we love you.

A., R., A. and T. B.

August 13th, 2009

Uncle Ken, as others have already said, please don't feel like you need to apologize for crying. This battle you are fighting is a hard battle and it is okay to have whatever emotions you need to deal with what you are feeling. Mad, sad, happy, anything you are feeling, you can share that with us. We will love you, support you, get angry with you, cry with you and laugh with you. You never have to feel like that isn't okay. This too is a safe place for you.

There is nothing selfish about what you want. Those are things in your life that have been important to you, things that you have invested time and love into.

You are a very strong man who is loved, respected and admired. You are also a man who is surrounded by a lot of people who can't carry the burden for you but won't let you walk through it by yourself. You are in our thoughts and prayers. We will pray for you to get ahead of the pain. I love you!

A. R.

August 13th, 2009

Ken, it's hard for me to come up with the words to relate how I feel. I have always respected you as a manager, and even more so as a person. Without you and your encouraging words, I would have never increased my level of care or pursued the jobs that I have now. You have been one of the strongest people that I know of and all around you should take this chapter out of your book and apply it to their lives. I want you to know that I'm here for you. Thank you for being you! Be strong!

B. C.

August 14th, 2009

You are in our prayers, and I hope it gets easier.

J. B.

August 14th, 2009

Hello Sir! Just wanted you to know that you are in my thoughts and prayers every day. The whole crying thing I have learned is a good thing. I too have been crying for many months. You will get through all of this. The good Lord has plans for you here. It was so wonderful to see you at the picnic Saturday. You look wonderful. I enjoyed talking to you very, very much. You are someone who can relate to things that I too have been going through, and to talk to you was very comforting. Please call me anytime day or night if you need someone there just to talk or listen. Believe me, there will be those days.

As we said at the picnic, Sir, every day is a blessing. You can only take one day at a time and enjoy it. I miss you, Sir!

D. P.

August 14th, 2009

Ken, you are more of a man to cry. It shows that you have feelings and you have a caring heart. Never be ashamed to cry. We all feel your pain, and I pray for you every day. You mean the world to me and others. Never forget that. We all love you and hope the best for your health.

Always a friend,
K. H.

August 15th, 2009

Bossman, there are no words to speak of what you are going through. Though I have only been a small part of the FLA family and your family for the last almost seven years, I remember when I first interviewed at FLA for an EMT position. When I first met you, I was sooo intimidated. To watch you walk and carry yourself with such poise. I know you have always portrayed that image. I cannot begin to understand the mental world war that you are going through. I can only tell you how much my wife and I love and care about you and Mickie. I know that, yes, you do have a very special place in our hearts. There is not a day that goes by that I don't think about you and what you are going through. I remember a time when I was ready to quit EMS all together and look for a different job.

Then I am reminded of a stout General Manager at FLA who looked at me and said, "Forget that crap. We are going to get you through this C". I know this pales very much in contrast with what you are going through. I just want you to know it was you who pushed me to strive for better things for myself in EMS. It was you who wouldn't let me quit or get down on myself when I got frustrated. I have come to know you as *way more* than just my employer. You have improved upon my abilities as a professional in EMS. I now strive even more than before to show that I am the product of the *Ken Kelly* medic teachings. I am the medic today because of *you*. I am always here for you and Mickiebear. I say prayers for you every day. I know you are retired military, so I know you will understand this: *don't give it the satisfaction*! My phone is on 24-7 for you and Mickie, no matter what. Say the word, and I will be wherever you need me to be. I don't care what time, day or night. You and Mickiebear are forever a big part of my family. Know that we love you and are here.

C. N.

August 15th, 2009

I am saying prayers for you and your doctors. I also want to tell you the secret that all women know. We cry because it makes us feel better and makes us stronger. That is the reason that women live longer. Crying doesn't make you weaker. It makes you stronger and it strengthens your heart and your blood pressure. I am thinking about you.

J. D.

August 16th, 2009

M. D. led me here. We are both Chamber Ambassadors, and she is always pleasant. I found out at one of the meetings that she was associated with FLA and I asked if she knew you. Of course, I know you from Star Market, backing into that space with my cookie truck on Main Street, Canandaigua, the back dock at Wegman's and the backyard of our old home after our neighbor had a stroke. You always show up when someone is in dire need of an EMT. I would like to visit with you sometime. You write about angels! You are one, but only a few of us know that. But HE knows, and that's important, so keep the faith, man!

J. K.

August 18ᵗʰ, 2009

Hello Ken. There is no shame in crying. We all, family and friends alike, cry with you. Please know that you and Mickie are constantly in our thoughts and prayers.

We love you,
E. and K. K.

August 19ᵗʰ, 2009

I was sitting here reading what everyone wrote to you and have to realize how many love you and pray for you on a daily basis. This has to make you feel good and strong. I remember all the good times we had in Canandaigua. You were not only my crew chief and boss, but you are my friend. My kids called your mom Grandma. I feel like we are like family. I can talk to you without being intimidated like others. Remember I am an army brat, and anything you threw at me, I would come back with an answer. You have a beautiful wife with an extended family. Be happy and get better. We all love you. I pray for you every day.

I love you Ken.

K. H.

August 19ᵗʰ, 2009

Outstanding! You deserve some rest from the beast! Keep up the great fight. Thinking and praying for you daily. God bless.

K. G.

August 19ᵗʰ, 2009

Yeah! Miracles come one day at a time, don't they?
Love you.

J. F. F.

August 19ᵗʰ, 2009

Our dear Ken, we are sooo happy to hear this. We all can say that some prayers are being heard. E. loves you dearly as we all do. Love and prayers to you both.

E. and K. K.

August 19ᵗʰ, 2009

Uncle Ken, great news that these new meds are working for you and so happy you feel renewed. I hope this rejuvenation keeps your beast at bay for a long, long time (if not indefinitely). We'll continue to pray for this and for you.

We love you, think and pray for you each day.

All our love,
A., R., A. and T. B.

August 19th, 2009

Dear Ken, it brings me such joy that you are feeling better. These are the gifts that we hope for. You have always lived your life to the fullest and been grateful to our Creator. He is rewarding you and freeing you from pain and suffering. He is merciful. You, my friend, have an abundance of days ahead of you that are yours for the taking. If you can't fit them all into one pocket, let me know. I'll fill mine up for you too! I love you, my friend.

L. Y.

August 20th, 2009

Hey, Bossman, it was nice to see you this morning on my off-going shift smiling and joking as usual. I am glad that the new medicine is working for you. Take it easy today as I know how that goes. Stay safe and my daughter said to say, "What up, Bossman!" LOL.

C. N.

August 20th, 2009

Ken, I just found out about you. My thoughts and prayers are with you. May God keep you and Mickie in His loving hands during your time of trouble.

C. S.

August 28th, 2009

Ken, just catching up after a week away and a week of starting the fall semester. Glad to hear the meds are working and pray they are still working now more than a week later. It was great to see you a couple of weeks ago. Keep your spirits up and I will continue praying for your strength to battle the monster. Remember there is always a warm place for you to rest and visit.

C. C.

August 29th, 2009

Ken, one day at a time, one little step at a time and one single prayer at a time. Nothing is impossible.

S. and R. T.

August 29th, 2009

Hello KWK. That is just awesome news. I love that you are feeling renewed. More good days then bad ahead my dear friend. XO.

L. M. Y.

August 29th, 2009

Hey, Bossman, that is good to hear that you are feeling better. I know that you will have some bad ones ahead too. But know that you have an enormous number of friends and family that are here for you in whatever capacity we are needed for. Know also that the Big Dog upstairs has a plan for all of us. Just like you said, "Seize the day". Make of it what you want or need. Enjoy the rest of your weekend. *Happy anniversary, my friend.*

C. N.

August 29th, 2009

Hello Sir! I am so happy that you are starting to feel a little better! I think about you every day and think how much of an amazing and strong person you are. I love to see that you are kicking the beast's butt! Hang in there and take every day for what it's worth. Remember how much your friends and family love you. I will always be here for you for anything you ever need. You can even borrow my wheelchair anytime that you feel tired. LOL. I would rather go without it and let you use it than to see you in pain, Sir. You have been a huge inspiration to me through my times of pain. Thank you, Sir! Will keep you in my prayers and thoughts daily.

D. P.

August 29th, 2009

Uncle Ken, it is wonderful to hear that you are feeling good and that your treatment was not hard on you. I hope you had a nice anniversary. Happy Fifth! I think of you every day, and I am thankful that I can be overjoyed with you as well. I will continue to pray for you.

A. R.

August 30th, 2009

Hey, Ken, just read your Saturday update. What a great report! So happy for you. You and Mickie are continually in my thoughts and prayers.

J. D.

August 30th, 2009

So happy you are sleeping better. Praying this treatment will last and you will keep feeling well. We are praying everyday for you.

T. K.

September 3rd, 2009

Uncle Ken, we just got back from dropping T. off at college. She was so happy she got to visit with you before she left. It meant a lot to her. I am so happy to read that this treatment is working for you and will pray that it continues.

I hope you and Mickie get to celebrate many more years together! Happy Anniversary! We love you.

A. and R. B.

September 2nd, 2009

Great news! Saturday's report is awesome and we will keep you in our prayers.

C. C.

September 3rd, 2009

Ken, keep the faith! We will keep you and Mickie in our prayers.

B. and R. G.

September 3rd, 2009

Now, that is the Ken I know. Hang in there. You are a fighter. You have to be strong and fight this thing that is trying to take over your body. My prayers are with you every day.

K. H.

September 3rd, 2009

Hi Kenny, it is amazing to see what a delicate balance our bodies generate in creating health. So glad you are feeling better, even though maybe confused? I would be. I hope you are enjoying this beautiful moment. The weather has been so glorious. And good luck with the next set of experts, advices and questions. I hope they can find an answer for the flank pain. Glad your spirits are high. That is 90 percent of the battle.

Love you,
J. F. F.

September 4th, 2009

Ken, glad you are not as sick as you thought you would be this time around. We will pray all the doctor visits will show what is going on so they can help with the pain or tell you how to ease it. Thank you for being open with all of us that care and love you. It really does help us to direct our prayers in the right direction for you.

Love,
T. and S. K.

September 4th, 2009

Dear Ken, you are very strong. We are praying for you and Mickie every day. Staying on top of that thing is the most important. We love you dearly.

K. and E. K.

September 4th, 2009

Uncle Ken, at this point, there always seems to be mixed news. But looking back, your news has been getting more positive than negative. Eventually you *will* receive only positive feedback. You seem to be feeling better more often than not and your attitude is a positive, fighting one. This is key in this fight because the beast you are fighting is only negative, and we all know where negative attitudes get us.

You have, again, shown us the strength you possess; and we are proud that you continue to lead this battle. We continue to pray for you, and there is no expiration on the offer to help, if you so need. We love you.

A. and R. B.

September 5ᵗʰ, 2009

Hi Kenny and Mickie. This will be a quickie because I've got so much business stuff to deal with before I go to bed. That's kind of an oxymoron though. *You* are important to me. More important than business and all which when we all become "dust in the wind". The bottom line is love, family and friends are what is #1. Right now *you* are #1 on my mind.

I had such a great time at J. and B.'s anniversary party, and I'm sooo glad you two were able to attend with S. and T. What an awesome network you have in your own family circle. It was a nice celebration of love and life, wasn't it?

Please take good care. Know that lots of love and support are coming your way and to the whole family too. May God bless!

PS Since you are in the medical business, can I ask you a question? I saw this show the other night, and I think I might have a case of sickle cell anemia. I have all the symptoms like we talked about at the anniversary party. What do you think? Ha ha ha! Lots of love to you all always.

K. L. H.

September 5ᵗʰ, 2009

Dear Kenny, please know I do not mean to offend anyone, just being "blond" and joking! (About my latest disease that I think I may have!) Please forgive me if I have offended anyone. The glass is always more than half full rather than half empty. J. has hooked me up with TUT.com with thoughts from the universe and daily blurbs that help to reinforce our positive thoughts. "Thoughts are things, what you think about you talk about, what you talk about you bring about". J. has been telling me that for years, and you know what? She is right. Stay in the positive. If you have a chance, check it out www. tut.com. I think that's the website, but J. will know for sure.

Again, thoughts are things. Choose the good ones!

Much love and blessings always,
Your blondie Cuz, K. L. H.

September 8ᵗʰ, 2009

Dear Ken, I think you are being strong enough for all of us. The words are sometimes hard to find. But kick back, have a beer, keep smiling and always remember we are all there for you.

D. O.

September 9ᵗʰ, 2009

Sorry to hear you had such a bad day. We are here for you and we all will continue to pray for you.

T. K.

September 9ᵗʰ, 2009

UK (that sounds very distinguished, like you and like the very resilient country that has been able to maintain and overcome many adversities), I believe in you and your strength and am here for you no matter what. This is just a minor setback in the big battle. You will overcome, if not by your own strength but from the strength of all of us combined, because we all believe in your will power and strength.

Carpe diem! Keep up the willpower because we are!

Love you,
A. and R. B.

September 10ᵗʰ, 2009

Stay strong and keep fighting. You are with us in our thoughts and prayers. Glad you are keeping up with the battle.

A. K. and C. D.

September 11ᵗʰ, 2009

Ken, remember, when you smile, we all smile. When you are in pain, we all feel the pain. If you stumble, we will hold you up. You are not alone. You have touched the hearts of many and we are all there for you.

D. O.

September 11ᵗʰ, 2009

Sir, I am so glad you are having a great day! I hope there are many more days like today. It brings such joy to me when I read good news about you. Keep strong. Have an awesome weekend. My family and I keep you in our thoughts and prayers every day.

D. P.

September 11ᵗʰ, 2009

Ken, I am glad to hear you are feeling good. The laughter that has filled the office this week has told me that the beast is away. Keep the great job up!

L. C.

September 11ᵗʰ, 2009

Yeah! So glad you are getting some relief.

Love you,
J. F. F.

September 11ᵗʰ, 2009

Ken, it is awesome that you are having a great day. I hope you have many, many more great days. Stay strong, and as always, you are in our thoughts and prayers.

B. and R. G.

September 11ᵗʰ, 2009

Ken, so glad you are feeling well today as I was worried how you would feel after your class. We are praying and will keep on until the beast is gone.

Love,
S. and T. K.

September 11ᵗʰ, 2009

Awesome news today and relieved to hear your pain is under control. We'll keep the prayers coming.

C. C.

September 15ᵗʰ, 2009

Hi Kenny and family, I'm so glad you are doing better. All of us that love and care about you, your journey is our journey. You give us strength, love and "eye openers". Love is what it's all about, and everyone who loves you sends it over and over along with lots and lots of prayers. What a blessing this avenue (Caring Bridge) is for everyone. You are in my heart, prayers and thoughts. Hang in there, Kiddo! You've got the "white light" around you so thick and strong. All I can say is "*Wow!*"

Lots and lots of love,
Your blondie Cuz, K. L. H.

Thank you for opening my eyes and for bringing us all together. Life is short, and love is what it is all about. God bless.

K. L. H.

September 18ᵗʰ, 2009

I have been thinking about you a lot, and I was glad to see that you are not having the pain. This weekend is supposed to be beautiful. Take it easy and enjoy it!

Love you,
A. R.

September 20th, 2009

Hi Ken. I'm so sorry to hear you are having such difficult health problems. I have another friend too who is battling cancer, and he has already doubled his time by keeping up the good fight. He has brain cancer, so I know it is possible to fight the beast and keep it at bay.

D. and I are thinking of you and Mickie and sending you our prayers. If you or Mickie ever need anything at all, please make sure you call us.

Love,
B. and D. P.

September 26th, 2009

Hello! I hope you are having a wonderful time with T. and J.! It was wonderful to see your spirits so high the other day. It is truly a gift the friendship you have with them and it made me happy to see that the upcoming visit made you "glow". I think of you often.

Love,
A. R.

September 29th, 2009

We are still praying for you. Maybe I can get you some cookies. They always make things better.

S. P.

September 29th, 2009

I have asked why things have happened to me and I have made peace with accepting as fact that everything happens for a reason. That thought crosses my mind each and every morning before my feet even hit the floor. I am looking forward to the day when I am able to comprehend just what those reasons are. Until then, I have no choice but to believe that there is a "big picture" that I am not able to bring into focus at this time. When I do, the vision will be glorious and grand.

You are an inspiration to so many in so many different ways. Your greatest ally in this battle is your faith and the tremendous network of love and support that you have spent your lifetime developing by simply being who you are and doing what you do. Lean on us for whatever you need. We're here for a reason.

J. R. M.

September 29ᵗʰ, 2009

Our dearest Ken, you have the right to feel you are squeezing Jesus's hand too tight. He has had you here to squeeze so many others hands, and now it is your turn. We hope that you will have brighter days ahead and soon. If there is anything we can do or if you wish to squeeze our hands, they are there for you. If you want to just call and vent, we are here. A prayer or ten are always being said for you. We love you and wish that we could take your legs and you have ours.

Love forever,
E. and K. K.

September 29ᵗʰ, 2009

Dearest brother Ken, I cannot begin to imagine what you are thinking, feeling or going through with your battle. I do believe that there is no such thing as holding on to Jesus too tightly. Who better to hold on to? He is always there, even when we think we are completely alone. I wish there was something I could do or say to assuage your pain and fears. I can tell you that we are here for you any time, day or night. Just call if you need to talk or whatever you need. You have been the rock of our family for years and I have the utmost respect and admiration for you. I love you, Brother. I hope, in my lifetime, that I can do just a tiny fraction of the good that you have done. Your heavenly reward will be greater than all the treasures on earth, of that I am sure.

E. K.

September 29ᵗʰ, 2009

Ken, it is okay for you to feel down. We all do even when we aren't going through what you are going through. You have tried to be strong in front of your family and friends. We are proud of you for that, but we are here to carry you if need be. We are here to hold your hand, and we are also here to cry with you if you need us to. That is what family and friends are all about. We are so happy that you feel that Jesus is holding your hand. You can never hold on too tightly because He is there every step of the way. In the past couple of weeks as I prayed for you, I thought about the verses of "Footprints in the Sand" written by Mary Stevenson. It applies to you! God bless.

T. K.

September 29ᵗʰ, 2009

There will never be a need to ask. Your "family" will always walk beside you. It is okay to be sad, Ken. We are all here for you, and phones are always on, and doors are always open. Keep smiling, Ken. That's how I know you are okay.

L. C.

September 29ᵗʰ, 2009

Uncle Ken, I have been thinking a lot about you these past couple of weeks and am glad to know that you were enjoying yourself with your friends and not feeling too bad. I am sorry things aren't going so well today but am comforted to know that you are still hold-ing the hand of Jesus. I wouldn't worry about holding His hand too tightly. I believe the tighter we hold, the happier He is and especially times like this. If you feel you have too tight of a grip, always know you have family and friends that are also willing to share in the hand holding. Also know it will never seem too tight of a grip, no matter how tight you feel you are holding on. I continue to pray for you and hope the neurologist will be able to help in the leg issue.

Although this all sounds redundant, the fact is, we all love you and are willing to do anything for you. Don't hesitate to take any of us up on the offer because you know that any one of us will respond on yesterday's time!

All our love,
A. and R. B.

September 29th, 2009

Ken, have you ever heard about "Footprints in the Sand"? It's about having Jesus at your side even when you think He isn't. He is there. Sometimes we think we are going through the really toughest things in our lives alone. I want you to know that *you aren't alone*! Jesus is always there. That is why we sometimes only see one set of footprints in the sand. I have learned that when we think that way, it is Jesus's footprints in the sand carrying us and that is not a bad thing at all. No matter, I am willing to be there where ever you need me to be at whatever the time. I will be there physically and in spirit. Know that you and Mickie are a part of my family and *we love you both*!

C. N.

September 30th, 2009

Dear sweet Ken, you are always on my mind and in my prayers. Let me know if I can do anything to assuage your pain or fear. You are a good man and a great friend. I love you.

L. M. Y.

September 30th, 2009

Hey Ken, just wanted to let you know that I am thinking of you and praying for you. You can never squeeze His hand too tightly. The tighter you squeeze, the stronger He becomes. His strength is perfected in our weakness. Love you, bro!

J. D.

October 2nd, 2009

Ken, I hope that you have had good news from your doctor. It is amazing how He never complains when we lean a little or squeeze His hand too tightly. K. and I will keep you and your family in our prayers. If you or Mickie need anything, do not hesitate to call. My phone is always on.

P. H.

October 3rd, 2009

Hey Ken, I have been thinking about you and praying for you often. It is okay to look to the Lord and ask for His help. We all do it at one time or another. Those who truly accept Him, and themselves, are the ones who ask for Him the most. I hope to one day be as strong in my faith as you. As I have said before, even in your struggle, you are an inspiration to all you touch. You continue to teach me so much.

With all that being said, I am here for anything you need, as are the rest of your friends and family. We all love you and cherish you. God bless you.

With love and prayers,
J. H.

October 3rd, 2009

Ken, I could not have said this any better and with a tissue in hand, I say, "Thank you". Thank you for being an amazing person. For caring so much about your employees, your family, your friends, your patients, your students, and anyone else who has the pleasure of crossing your path! That has been my theory my entire life. I lost it for a while, but now I am back on track. What matters in life is what is important to you and not what everyone else thinks. If the entire world would realize this, everyone would be so much happier.

So enjoy the day as it is a nice sunny one. Perfect for riding. Carpe diem, Sir!

J. B.

October 3rd, 2009

Ken, you are the most unselfish person I know. You have given a lot to others without asking for anything in return. I have learned a lot from you; and I am the luckiest person to know you, your mom, A. and Mickie. You are like my extended family. I pray for you every day. I wish that I can be as strong as you are. For my favorite saying, "Stay safe and take care." Eat those cookies.

Love you, Ken.

K. H.

October 3rd, 2009

My dearest Ken, words escape me, I think, which is a dangerous thing for me to be doing. Regardless of that, you continue to amaze me and inspire me. You and your family are always in our prayers. May God bless and keep you in His loving hands.

All our love,
S. and R. T.

October 4th, 2009

Hey Cuz, just got home from a week on the road trying to see color in Vermont where gray seemed to predominate. Still a nice trip to a very pretty place. You have been on my mind. I am sorry the dark moments have been so strong. The gray does invade our psyche too and I know it's been gray here. The attitude of gratitude is a big help. So are cookies and lots of chocolate ice cream. Unmade beds *rule*!

It's so hard to be vulnerable. It's so hard to feel lousy. None of us have any guarantees, and all we can do is make the best of today. Laugh a little, love a lot, pet a dog, kiss a kid, hug your loved ones, and dust your lions. It takes a lot to learn to be alive in this moment, as that is all any of us have. My wish for you is to be alive in this moment, then let it go and be alive in the next one. Eat your cookies! I love you.

J. F. F.

October 4th, 2009

My friend, you continue to amaze me. I learn from you every day. Now, as I wipe the tears, I will make us some cookies to enjoy in the morning. There for you always.

D. O.

October 4th, 2009

Uncle Ken, kudos to you! I love you so much, I can't even begin to express how much. R. just got home and got a new toy for his jeep, an air raid siren, because you know every 1952 Willy's Jeep needs one of those! At least your cookies won't bother the neighbors!

Indulge yourself in any and every way you can. If you run out of ideas, I'm sure the great minds that surround you can come up with something!

Keep the faith, as we all are.

Love,
A. and R. B.

October 4th, 2009

Mr. Kelly, hello, Sir, I just want you to know that you have touched so many lives, especially mine. Through all I have gone through, you seem to always be there for me. I hope I can do the same for you now. You are in my thoughts and prayers daily. I really hope to get a chance to see you this week. If there is anything I can do for you, please do not hesitate. Take care and remember how much I love you.

Your friend forever,
D. P.

October 4th, 2009

Dear Ken, it's very simple, you have brought nothing but joy, love and laughter to my life. So when you are feeling blue, remember flipping over in the rocking chair and flinging your pizza all over the wall and my white carpeting. Best pizza moment ever!

I love you. XOXOXO.

L. Y.

October 5th, 2009

Dear Ken, I don't know where to begin. When you first interviewed me for a position at FLA, I was as nervous as all got out and I didn't know what to expect. Then through the years, I found you to be not only an inspiration but someone who sees potential in everyone you connect with. I remember you asking me why was I going into the CC (critical care) program when I needed to take the paramedic instead. You did not know me well then, but I guess you had that uncanny instinct of seeing my potential even if I didn't. It took some time, but I did take your paramedic class and am a better person for doing so. I have learned so many things from you and still continue to learn. If I can be a half, no, even a quarter of the paramedic that you are, then I have given to my patients something of great value. I write this after reading your recent journal entry with a heavy heart and several tears in my eyes. It's a good thing I don't have to see to type.

May God bless you and all your many friends, as you have blessed us. I look forward to seeing you at the "Vital Signs" conference.

With great care,
E. and C. A.

October 6th, 2009

Out of darkness comes light. Thank you for the reminder of life. While working Pediatric Hematology Oncology, I was reminded every day how precious our lives are and to always live to the fullest. Occasionally, we all need a reminder as to why we are here and to count our many blessings that the Lord has bestowed upon us. Your grace is an inspiration to me. I am sure your restful weekend has lifted some of the darkness of last week. My prayers for you continue. Enjoy your celebrity at "Vital Signs".

C. C.

October 7ᵗʰ, 2009

Ken, what a beautiful message you have given to all of us. You really have a gift for writing. I too have given up caring what others think about me or the things I choose in my days. Thank you for all the EMT classes you have taught. I have enjoyed being an EMT more than most other things in my life, except maybe being a mom.

We are all here for you and Mickie, whatever and whenever you need it. I include you and your family in my prayers and I know that you never walk alone.

B. S. P.

October 7ᵗʰ, 2009

Uncle Ken, when I read your last entry, I cried. You have been such an important part of my life. My uncle, my neighbor, Grandma's caregiver, my parents' close friend, and now I am proud to call you my friend too. You have the love and respect of so many. The thing that makes that so much more special is you don't demand it. You get that by living as a good man. That is what you are, a very good man.

I am sorry to hear that you are having a hard time right now. You are in my thoughts and prayers every day. If you need cookies, there are three little ones who love delivering them. If you make a mess, well, I know a cleaning lady or two. Buy those things that you want and stay up late. As far as the shirt, I think you have always gone without that at the beach or not. If you need to laugh, we all have stories. If you need to cry, we can cry with you. If you feel alone, you can always meet us here.

Love,
A. R.

October 12ᵗʰ, 2009

Ken, your cookies don't have to be Archway either. Your October 3ʳᵈ entry was sad and inspiring. I'm saving it in a special "Inspiration and Wisdom" folder so I can reread it, reflect and reread it again. The origin of your thoughts is obvious. Keep writing them when you can.

J. K.

October 12ᵗʰ, 2009

Dear Kenny, I'm so sorry you are having a tough time. The journaling of your feelings is an amazing gift and a reminder to us all about savoring the moment. Life is short and we tend to get caught up in daily things and forget how precious life is. I'm glad you are being easier on yourself. Have at all the cookies and whatever else you want. You've more than earned it. You are in my thoughts and prayers daily. God bless you and may He make this journey easier for you.

Lots of love always,
K. L. H.

October 19ᵗʰ, 2009

Hello Sir! I want to congratulate you for the award you received this past weekend! However, I do have to say, I believe it is way over-due. I hope all the tests come back negative for you. Like always, I will think about you every day and pray for you! I miss you and Mickie so much. Hope you both have an amazing great week.

D. P.

October 19th, 2009

Dear Ken, I love you very much. I am here for you. My son worships and adores you. Keep the faith. Lean on us. We will be the ones who will hang the sun high, make the oceans have waves, give the roses their smell—anything to make you smile. We are your people, and our love for you is pure. You are the best man I know.

Love,
L. M. Y.

October 19th, 2009

Ken, I work for the American Red Cross. I donate double reds, which is two units of just red blood cells. This is for cancer patients that have a low count. To everyone that reads this, I ask that you find a blood drive and donate. If you are O+, O-, A- or B- donate double reds. Do this for Ken and anyone you know that has cancer. Ken, keep your head up. We all love you and wish and pray for the best for you.

K. H.

October 19th, 2009

Uncle Ken, I love you so much and I really hope that everything is getting better. I'll be praying for you up here and I can't wait to see you when I get home for Christmas. I don't have my own account, so I'm using my mother's. I do care so much, and I love you so much. You are always in my thoughts. I love you!

T. B.

October 20th, 2009

Uncle Ken, it was an honor and privilege to see you receive your award! I am glad that you were able to have that time without the beast. We are praying for you!

Love,
A. R.

October 21st, 2009

Dear Ken, what a wonderful recognition you received this past weekend. As a student of your teachings, I can honestly say that we are the ones who have been honored by you. Your knowledge, your true passion for the workings of the mind and body and your utmost love of all God's gifts leaves me in total awe. This dreadful beast dares not attempt to take who you are. It just can't. It will not be allowed. You are fierce and mighty with the warriors of love that you have with you at all times.

Love,
L. M. Y.

October 21st, 2009

Uncle Ken, congratulations on your award. It warms my heart that you were recognized not only by your peers but by the state of New York for a job you are so passionate about and also that you were able to share that with your family and friends. Although you have been told numerous times of the difference you have made in your student and coworker's lives, sometimes you don't believe or recognize how much of a difference you have made until you are officially recognized. It is a good feeling to be recognized for a job well done. So happy for you and so well deserved!

I'm glad to hear you are still able to keep the pain under control and have some knowledge of what is causing it. You know what they say, knowledge is power. I continue to pray for you every day and will pray even harder that these found tumors won't spread any farther than what they have already.

R. and I enjoyed having you and Mickie for dinner and are looking forward to the next gathering.

Love,
A. B.

October 21ˢᵗ, 2009

Ken after reading all of your posts, I have wanted to but never know what to write or respond. Yes, me at a loss for words! I have known you for many years and have seen your caring and the difference you have made in many people's lives. I send this note with love and caring to you and Mickie and say thank you to both of you for being *you*!

B. M. (A.)

October 21ˢᵗ, 2009

Ken, the beast knows not who he is fighting! You are and always have been a very strong-natured person. While I read with sorrow your most recent post, it is strength from Him that will guide us all in this trek along life. My prayers for your comfort and peace are a daily occurrence, as well as two prayer groups that I have direct knowledge of. Love and best wishes to you and Mickie.

P. and K. H.

October 24th, 2009

Mr. Kelly, it is always a pleasure to come to class and hear your lectures. I wish nothing but pain-free days for you and know that our class is very fortunate to have you as our Paramedic Instructor.

Always,
L. K.

October 30th, 2009

Uncle Ken, I have been thinking about you a lot these last couple of days. I just wanted to let you know that. I hope you are having a great day!

Love,
A. R.

November 3rd, 2009

Hi Kenny, I have been laid low for two weeks with the flu but want to belatedly offer my congratulations on the wonderful award that you were given. Couldn't have been to a better choice. I am so proud to be related to you. I also want to offer my support, love and prayers regarding the MRI (magnetic resonance imaging) outcome. I am holding you and Mickie in my heart. I love you.

J. F. F.

November 5th, 2009

Okay, so about the cookies! When was it that you worried about how many cookies you ate?

B. S.

November 5th, 2009

Hi Ken. I saw J. K. at voting Tuesday, and he told me of your problem. That's something I didn't want to hear. You've always been such a strong and caring person. You have helped me in so many ways while I was going through some tough times. I really need to tell you that I'm doing ever so much better. Like M. says, "My shy little friend has turned into a social butterfly". I'm also a great grandmother now. It sounds like you are keeping your chin up and are in the hands of the Lord. I really wanted you to know how much I care and will keep you in my prayers.

E. A.

November 6th, 2009

Mr. Kelly, again, you have managed to bring tears to my eyes. I continually am amazed by your strength, resolve and your faith. Here, in your pain and struggle, you are still teaching us that we have a purpose in the darkest of hours. Teaching us that strength is still possible, that faith can grow stronger and that your love for your fellow man is still there.

Every day that I come to work and see you there, I strive to be a better person, a better husband, a better father and certainly a better paramedic. I am very proud to say that I am a Ken Kelly Paramedic.

R. T.

November 6th, 2009

Mr. Kelly, you continue to awe and inspire me as you fight and stand up against the beast. Even as you deal with the tendrils that continue to try and reach out, you continue to hold a perspective toward bettering mankind. You, Sir, are a very strong man. My hope is that, as you stated, your fight will become a benefit to others. I don't believe I could be as strong as you are. You have such a strength, such a strong hold on your faith that no one can match that. God bless you, Sir, and continue to fight that beast. You, Mickie and your family are in my thoughts each and every day. You continue to make me proud to not only work for you, but simply to know you. That has made me more appreciative of the day-to-day things we so often take for granted. You continue to be an inspiration to many, myself included.

M. G.

November 6th, 2009

Ken, after reading your message, I can see you getting through to the two people who took their lives. You have inspired a lot of people and I am very proud of you. You are a good friend and always will be. I pray for you every day. Remember, you have made a big influence on everyone you come in contact with. Continue doing that—be strong and you will overcome this beast.

Love,
K. H.

November 6th, 2009

You are such a blessing in my life. I love you.

J. F. F.

November 6th, 2009

As always Ken, you are thinking of others before yourself; and that is one of your very endearing qualities. Keep fighting as you are very loved my many!

J. B.

November 7th, 2009

Uncle Ken, well said. We will always be here for you.

Love,
A. and R. B.

November 7th, 2009

Ken, after reading your note today I can truly say, you have a heart for people, and the way you treat them is why you do what you do for a living. I could see you talking to people and calming their fears. It is true that life here is just the beginning to what is after this life. You will receive a few crowns in Heaven for all you have given to us here on earth. We all will face that time, whether it be by a beast or quick as lightning, we will face it. I pray that when I'm faced with any of life's testing, I will be as strong as you have shown yourself to be. Not just in the strength you have shown, but in the frailness, you have shared with us all. You are an example to all. We have all been so proud to be a part of your life before this all happened. Now, and even after, we all will carry you in our prayers, in our hearts and even in our arms. You are in my thoughts and prayers daily.

T. K.

November 7th, 2009

Hi, Kenny, I want you to know you are in my thoughts and prayers every day. Congratulations on your award! You are an amazing man. I'm sorry that the beast continues to test you and give you pain. You know you are surrounded by the love of family and friends, and all of our prayers are to protect you and surround you with the white light and keep the beast at bay. I'm so proud to be a part of your family. I love you and am sending lots of love and healing energy your way.

K. L. H.

November 9th, 2009

Well, I am glad you set us straight. I was getting concerned and I was ready to remove your scissors and stapler from your office. Yes, we are here for you at all times, and there will always be an extra cookie at your side.

D. O.

November 16th, 2009

Ken, I just want you to know that we are here for you and that we are praying for you. You do so much for others and ask for nothing in return. I am grateful for your wisdom regarding E. and the whole autism thing and educating others. I have only known you a few short years, but in that time, I have come to respect you very much and I value your input. I know our lives are better having known you. The world could use a few more Ken Kellys. Hang in there! Call us if you need us!

D. and G. Y.

November 17th, 2009

Mr. Kelly, I can't follow your blogs any longer without saying my piece. I just want to say that I am really thankful that I got the chance to know you. Through my rough times at FLA, you were there. Although I was very much intimidated by you at first, I soon realized you weren't only my employer, but there as my friend. There were a few times when I needed someone to talk to, and yet I never sought anyone out. You knew. You told me I wasn't leaving work until we talked about things. Your words of kindness and the fact of knowing you were there for me and everyone else that has ever been under that roof made the difference. I can now look back on my experience at FLA with a smile because I was able to know many people that in all made a family. I pray for you daily and wish I could pop in and offer to take you and the Mrs. out to lunch. Maybe after the holidays, we can visit. I really miss it there and would give almost anything to come back. Best wishes to you and your family. Please tell Mrs. Kelly that I said hi and that I miss her as well. Hope to talk and see you soon. Happy Holidays.

S. S.

November 17th, 2009

November 17th, 2009

Mr. Kelly, a smile is on my face today as it was late last week when you and I were on the phone. My daughter was on her way to work and I said, "I love you". In your wit, you asked if I was saying that to you and we both laughed. Laughter is good and although I was saying "I love you" to my daughter, you must know that I love you as well.

By the way, thank you for your help this morning.

R. T.

November 17th, 2009

I am so tickled that the mismatched and wild-colored socks made you happy! They are to wear when eating cookies on days you don't make the bed and when you sit with your elegant lions on the front porch. I am wearing mine too! Wouldn't your mom and grandma smile? Thanks for the family photo too. You look so handsome in your uniform! Sending a big hug to go along with the mismatched and wild-color combination socks! I am also so happy that the treatment is helping! I vote for sunny days too.

Lots of love,
J. F. F.

November 17th, 2009

Hey Kenny and Mickie, crazy socks, eh? *Yup.* Leave it to my sister to come up with something unique to give you a smile! That's her! I'm so glad to hear that "the beast" is retreating for now. Isn't it amazing what love can do to help heal? I bet you two had fun with your crazy socks at work, wondering if anyone would notice and being the "bad kids out of uniform". Of course, if you didn't want them to notice they surely would have.

Hang in there, Kenny. You are awesome and so is the love surrounding you and Mickie. My prayers are for your good health, happiness and pain-free holidays!

Love,
Your Cuz, K.

Hey, have you been filling up on any cookies lately? Cookies, ice cream and sweets do amazing healing things. That huge sweet tooth runs in our family. Do you remember some of the awful stuff Grandma K. made? She was an amazing baker. I remember that she, Aunt S. and Uncle J. A. living across the street from us when we were growing up. They were a gift to all of us in my family. Ice cream and cookies, oh yeah! Oh, and yes, the sugarplum fairy is one of our favorites and here come the holidays. Savor and enjoy every bite that you can!

Lots of love always,
K. L. H.

November 20th, 2009

Ken, I just read some of your writing as I haven't received any for a while and had to reload. I think you should print your journal and publish it. I think it would be so comforting to other people going through what you are going through. It would also help all the friends and families who are trying to walk through this with their family member or friend. You sharing and us reading, I know for me, has helped me to understand what you are going through. Even though we can't change a thing, it does give us direction on what to pray for. You will be in my prayers today as always. We are just a phone call away. Thank you for sharing with all of us.

Love,
T. and S. K.

November 20th, 2009

Love you, Mr. Kelly!

R. T.

November 20th, 2009

The sun is shining just for you this morning. Even though I'm not with you—I am! A big hug is right here for you.

D. O.

November 20th, 2009

Kenny, Kenny, Kenny, you are awesome; and I'm sending you tons and tons of big bear hugs to help you through the process you are going through today. *Wow*, your list of things you love are wonderful, insightful, thoughtful and loving. You know what? Your journey is helping to awaken the rest of us around you to what is important. How many times do we stop and put down the things we love and the things we are grateful for? No, most of us get caught up in our everyday stress. Stop and smell the roses. When you are doing your chemo, breathe in deeply and slip into a deep sense of relaxation. Run the music and movies that have brought happiness and joy into your life. That's what is important, the love all around you and us all. Soak it in, relax, breathe in deeply (breathe out) and enjoy the memories. That is pure love and it also helps the medicine do its work. Remember, what you think about, you talk about, and what you talk about, you bring about. Thoughts are things, choose the good ones! A zillion big bear hugs and lots and lots of love coming your way.

Your Cuz, K.

PS Thank you so much for being such an important part of my life (and my family's lives) when we were younger and as we've grown older. Thank you for bringing us all back together closer again and for being the incredible person you are. You are so much like your mom, such a good and loving person. You remind me of her. You, Kenny, are an incredible person. Hang in there.

Love,
K. L. H.

November 20th, 2009

Mr. Kelly, I hope you've gotten a few hours of riding in today, brisk but nice! Your post is from the heart and that's why I loved it. Thank you for sharing, and hang in there. I will be making Christmas cookies soon. Chocolate chips are en route.

B. J. O.

November 20th, 2009

Uncle Ken, homemade mac and cheese is on its way. I was actually wishing to make that this weekend and now I know why! In fact, I just bought the ingredients yesterday on my way home from work. My girls always request this when they come home, so I hope you enjoy it as well.

I hope and pray this treatment is not as bad as it sounds to be, but if it is, know that you'll have all of those items on your list to look forward to and plenty of friends to provide for you while you are unable to provide for yourself.

We are here for you in every way. We love you, think about you and pray for you every day. It's okay to be scared, but less frightening when you know that others are there to help and share the burden with you. You truly are blessed with a multitude of angels and we are doubly blessed because of you.

Love,
A. and R. B.

November 20th, 2009

Ken, you are a blessing to us all.

M. D.

November 21st, 2009

Here comes a *big hug* for all those days.

Love,
J. F. F.

November 27th, 2009

Ken, after reading the letter you wrote today, my heart is so sad that you have to think this way. I also thank God for allowing us to be there for you. It was great having you, Mickie and family here on Thanksgiving Day. You are so much a part of our lives. You always bring joy to those around you, even in your battle with the beast. Thank you for being you. I pray God will bless you each day. God bless.

Love,
T. K.

November 27ᵗʰ, 2009

Your entry today about time really hits home. Yeah, I have a lot I want to get done and things that need to get or be done. One of those "need things" is my family and friends. I think I will be shutting off the computer after I post this and go play a game of checkers with Eric or maybe watch a Transformer movie with him.

Thanks Ken, for the "cyber kick" in the butt. You, my friend, are full of wisdom. Know you are loved and cared for by many. I could end this with the typical "Take care," but instead, I will close with this, "Take chances"!

D. Y.

November 27ᵗʰ, 2009

Ken, it's been a few years since we have seen each other, but I can still remember all the good times we shared. I wish that you didn't have to go through this, but I am a firm believer that God doesn't give us anything more than we can handle. You are a true inspiration to everyone that knows you. I feel very blessed to have known you for all these years. If there is anything that I can do, even if it is just a listening ear, feel free to contact me. You are one fabulous person.

M. B.

November 27ᵗʰ, 2009

Mr. Kelly, you have truly blessed and been a part of so many lives. Some of which I am sure you are not even aware of. I am very sorry that you are having to go through what you are. The beast is invading; however, I feel that with your positive attitude, you will have longer than that one year that you gave yourself. May God bless you during this terrible journey.

C. B.

November 27ᵗʰ, 2009

May God bless you, Ken. I will do the things that you suggest! Last week, when I was working, we took the call for the double homicide. I asked myself, like many others I'm sure, the question that has no answer: *Why!* My faith in our Lord is stronger than ever, and because of that, I am sure that, that little girl is in God's peace. I prayed for her, her mother and their families. I pray especially for the son (brother) and the father who will miss his little girl until they are united again. I prayed for your crew and all of the responders that had to see such a horrible crime scene. I went home that night instead of stopping at Gallagher's as I often do on a Friday night after work. My children and loving wife were all sleeping, but I didn't care. I was just happy to be home and thankful for my life and what I have. I said a prayer for you, my friend. I am thankful for all that you have done for me. I am a better person and a better EMT because of you! Thank you! Peace to you and Mickie.

S. D.

November 27ᵗʰ, 2009

Uncle Ken, I have been thinking about you a lot lately. I really wish we would have been able to spend time with you on Thanksgiving. It was very sad to know that I couldn't give you a hug I know you needed. We need to plan for us to all get together again after we are all healthy. I hope you have a wonderful weekend. We all love you!

Love,
L. C.

November 27ᵗʰ, 2009

Ken, this is truly a reawakening for me. It just reminds me of the friends I've lost through the years to the beast, some of whom I was very close to. I never knew how I felt or thought of them or never realized how much they meant to me until it was too late. I want you to know you are and have been in my prayers.

B. H.

November 27th, 2009

Ken, thank you for this sharing of you! You are truly an inspiration to us all. You have an amazing way with words. Hang tough and remember the "angel" in your pocket!

T. C.

November 27th, 2009

Hi Kenny, you certainly have a gift for powerful words to share with an important message that is too easy to forget or loose track of. Thank you for your best and worst. Your courage is inspiring for all. You are fortunate to have so many who love you. No need to apologize for the moments you use to vent. No one deserves it more. Thank you for being such a strong role model and teacher. All my love to you and Mickie.

L. B.

November 28th, 2009

You know, I have all these words that just pop up while I'm reading your postings and then I read what others say. Mmmmm, would my words be redundant? It doesn't matter as I smile to myself and continue to write regardless. Novel concept, that stopwatch! Implementation is another goal, yet one we should all consider. Consider it done!

I love you, Mr. Kelly, and thank you again!

R. T.

November 28th, 2009

Hi Kenny, wow, what a sobering thought about time that last entry of yours is. It is very good, and I am switching my priorities to family and the people who you love and who love you. They come first. I'm praying for peace on earth and for all of us to wake up and smell the roses (or coffee). It is so easy to get off track.

As D. T. says, "Never get sidetracked by less important tasks. Always focus on the goal. If you do get sidetracked, get right back on the rails, because ultimately sidetracking kills you".

Thanks for giving me the "wake up" call again. I somehow keep on slipping and getting caught up in other "stuff". I wish I were more disciplined, but then I know I'm the only one who can make that happen. Getting a "wake up" call or reminder from a loved one is sure a big help! My family and the people I love and care about are all that truly are important to me.

Hope you had a good Thanksgiving, and here's to a new stronger week. Thank you for sharing with that young boy about the "beast". I am sure you helped him a lot.

Lots and lots of love always,
K. L. H.

November 28th, 2009

I love you, Kenny.

J. F. F

November 28th, 2009

Hi Ken! I have been here many times to check on how you are doing. Each time I have left in tears, unable to share any thoughts or feelings that I may have. I kept telling myself, next time I'll leave some great inspirational words for you. Words that will make you feel better or get better or whatever. The next time I am still unable to do it. The very first time I met you, in the Poconos, you helped me. B. had slammed her finger in the door within minutes of us arriving and you were right there for us and you continue to help me. Because of you, I want to be a better person. I want to help just a fraction of the people you have helped. You are truly an amazing man and one I am honored to know. I now see life in a different way because of your journey and words. God bless you.

Love,
K. Y.

November 28th, 2009

Hi Ken and Mickie, this is R., K.'s mom. I am so happy to have gotten to know the two of you and hope to see you many more times! You are both in my prayers *every day*. Lots of love and prayers to you both.

R. K. Y.

November 28th, 2009

Mr. Kelly, so incredibly eloquent. I really hope you have saved a copy of every post because there is so much support and inspiration that comes from you. You are incredible and your strength amazes me. You make me a better person. I love you too, Ken.

B. J. O.

November 29th, 2009

Mr. Kelly, I am sorry that I have not visited before this point. While I have not known you for a long time, I have known you long enough for you to earn my utmost respect. Calm seas and good sailing!

Respectfully,
J. H.

November 29ᵗʰ, 2009

Mr. Kelly, I am so sorry to hear about that. You are a true warm-hearted person and a great boss. Well, take care.

M. B.

November 30ᵗʰ, 2009

Ken, you are in my thoughts and my prayers. I hope you know that if there is anything at all that I can do for you, all you have to do is ask. I am proud to call you my friend.

S. H.

December 4ᵗʰ, 2009

Dear Ken, thank you for sharing your journey with those who care deeply about you and Mickie. I pray each day that God continues to watch over you and keep you strong in your faith. Bless you.

S. W.

December 10ᵗʰ, 2009

Bask in the sun and cast your worries to the sea! Enjoy your trip.

JR and J. M.

December 10ᵗʰ, 2009

Ken, you are one of the strongest people that I know and it is okay to be scared, but do not give up. You will beat this beast. You go on vacation and enjoy yourself and don't have a care in the world. Put everything else out of your mind, then when you get home, go at it with full force. I just wish that I was even half the person that you are. All my prayers are with you beating this.

M. B.

December 10ᵗʰ, 2009

Ken, I have come and visited this site often and read your brave posts, but I never felt as though I knew the right words. I have not had the pleasure of knowing you for very long, but in ways you will never know, you have truly impacted *my life*. You had the belief that I could live my dream and have allowed me to practice my trade.

Every Friday, when I am able to do to temple, and the Rabbi asks us to name those of our family and friends who are in need of healing, I sadly voice your name.

Let the sand and the ocean take away your pain and enjoy the warm sun, sand and cold Coronas. Take care, Boss. You are always in my thoughts and prayers. God is watching out for all.

L. R. T.

December 10ᵗʰ, 2009

Ken, you go and enjoy the warm sun and the beautiful ocean. While the beast has reared his ugly head once again, you will be able to put it in check. We have faith in you.

P. H.

December 10ᵗʰ, 2009

Uncle Ken, there are so many people loving you and praying for you while you fight this. Your friends and family will be there for you always. Have a great time in Florida! Love you!

A. R.

December 10ᵗʰ, 2009

Uncle Ken, enjoy your long weekend in Florida, and I hope you will enjoy some nice weather also (at least better than what we have here). Have fun with your friends and laugh a lot. As if anyone can*not* laugh when they're with you, as you have such a wonderful sense of humor! Take a vacation, a true vacation from work, from snow, from alarm clocks and from worries. You know they'll be here when you get back. Unless, of course, you do feed that nasty alarm clock to the sharks!

I think you know by now that we are all here for you and praying for you no matter where you are or what you are doing.

Enjoy your vacation and let it be a true vacation. If you do find some sun, try to coax it home with you. We love you. Have a great time.

R. and A. B.

December 10ᵗʰ, 2009

Ken, this is normal. After all, you are human! You have many friends and family that love and care about you. One thing I've learned in my recovery of alcohol and addiction is that God won't give us any more than we can handle. Sometimes I find this hard to believe, but I remind myself of this when the rough spots pop up, I ask for His help to get me through.

B. H.

December 10ᵗʰ, 2009

How could you not be scared? I am glad you are going to grab some Florida sun as worrying won't make anything change. Fear of pain is the most human of all conditions, Kenny. I hear your strength and faith about the destination that sounds unshakeable. But the fear about the road ahead is so understandable. I wish I could take it away for you. I am so sorry. I am also praying for you and Mickie. I am sending you both big hugs to help you find your way through this hard news.

Lots of love,
J. F. F.

December 11ᵗʰ, 2009

Hi, Kenny and Mickie. Wow, I'm sorry to hear that the beast continues to haunt you and it's okay to be scared. Know that God never puts you into situations He knows in His heart you cannot handle, no matter what you think the lessons are. It is yours to choose to learn from them. I truly believe you are amazing at how well you are handling these challenges that have been given to you, and you are such an inspiration to all of us who love and care about you. We gather to surround you with lots of love.

Enjoy your time in Florida, take in all the beauty around you and know you are surrounded with lots of love and prayers for your health. God bless you both.

K. L. H.

December 11ᵗʰ, 2009

Ken, I know with this news you are having a hard time not thinking about the next step. Please try to just relax with Mickie and your friends in Florida and try to enjoy yourself. We are here for you. Remember we are available anytime. You are in our prayers always.

Love you,
T. and S. K.

December 11ᵗʰ, 2009

Ken, you are one of the strongest people I know. Being scared is normal. You have touched so many lives and have made each life that you have touched just that much better. You have a lot of people praying for you. Stay strong and enjoy the warm sands of Florida. Enjoy your trip.

D. and G. Y.

December 11ᵗʰ, 2009

Hello Sir! Well, I am very sorry to hear about the latest news! However, you are such a strong incredible man that I believe you will tackle this beast. However, I am very jealous that you are going to the nice warm area. I think you have picked a great weekend to go. Enjoy your time with Mickie and just relax.

Thank you again for being such an inspiration to me. I look up to you very much as a role model in my life. *So thank you!*

D. P.

December 11ᵗʰ, 2009

Mr. Kelly, to put it plain and simple, I am praying for you. Your news makes my heart ache. I think of you often and your battle with the beast. Please know that you are loved by so many. I pray that your journey is blessed with love, happiness and friendship.

C. B.

December 11ᵗʰ, 2009

Hi, Boss! I have always considered myself to be someone eloquent with words, but much like those times in paramedic school, you have me searching for something to say.

While I could essentially reiterate what I, and so many others have said previously, I will leave this to be a short and simple posting.

I am honored to be in your life and to have the opportunity to accompany you on this journey, as dismal as it seems at times. God does not give us challenges we cannot handle. For with faith, love, thanksgiving and the Lord's guidance and blessing, we can handle anything He gives us. While we may never know why these challenges are given to us, I think all of us who are faithful can understand that they make us stronger servants of the Lord.

With that being said, I am here for you, Ken and Mickie, as are so many others. Day or night I am here for you. Help around the house, an ear to talk to, a shoulder to cry on or someone to share a beer with—I am here.

All of us are on this journey with you, Ken. Enjoy your vacation for the days are always too short. As the tide ebbs and flows, let it take away your pain, sorrows and sadness. Take comfort and solace in the beauty the Lord has created. I continue to pray for you. God bless and love to you and your family.

J. H.

December 11th, 2009

L. and I will always be there for you. You have a great time on the beach. Big hugs always.

D. O.

December 11th, 2009

Uncle Ken, we are all here for you. I am making many yummy goodies for you when you return from your vacation! I hope you have a great vacation and truly get to relax. I love you and am always thinking and praying for you. Remember that you can always call if you need anything!

Love,
L. C.

December 12th, 2009

Hey Ken, I just read the latest. Know that I am praying for you and think of you and Mickie often. Enjoy your time at the beach!

J. D.

December 14th, 2009

Dear Ken, please know that you are always in our thoughts. Being scared of the unknown is part of being human. This is the "season of miracles" and we will pray for one for you. We hope you enjoyed your weekend in Florida and wish you a very Merry Christmas.

B., D. and D. P.

December 15th, 2009

Hey Bossman, I just read your update as I am holding my daughter in my arms. Talking with you has given me a whole new perspective about life, family and God. I want you to know how much it means to me to see you when I come back for end of shift at FLA. I have had several talks with you over the last few weeks, and it has helped immensely. I think about life in such a different way now. Since I have known you, you have always taught me to think about things in different ways. My family and I are here for you and Mickie in whatever capacity you need. We are only a phone call away, and my phone is on twenty-four hours a day. Our door is always open to you, Mickie and your family. God has blessed us with your pres-

KEN'S GREATEST CHALLENGE PART 2

ence, your caring and your understanding. We love you. I love you, Bossman!

C. N.

December 16th, 2009

Uncle Ken, I am glad you had a nice time in Florida. I think about you every day, and you are still in my daily prayers. I love you!

Love,
L. C.

December 16th, 2009

Hi Kenny, your love, faith, strong beliefs and strength in and from God continue to inspire, amaze and encourage me. I'm sure everyone around you, who loves and cares about you, feels the same way. You are amazing! I'm so glad you had a good time in Florida. It's interesting how a few days can change things, eh? You are a strong "rock of faith" that helps all of us who love you and believe in you become even stronger in our faith, prayers, hopes and wishes.

Now, if you happen to have an inside with God, can you ask Him to help me become a multimillionaire because I want to win the lottery? Huh? Just asking! Ha ha ha.

Lots of love,
K.

I'm leaving for NY tomorrow night and hope to see you over the holidays.

K. L. H.

December 17ᵗʰ, 2009

You are an amazing man, Mr. Kelly. Through your faith, you find strength, courage and are able to show your love for all of us. God has blessed you with attributes beyond belief and through Him you are blessing to us. Love you, Sir.

R. T.

December 19ᵗʰ, 2009

Ken, you are amazing to me. How, even in your battle with the beast, you encourage others. We are here for you always and in our prayers always. So happy your trip was relaxing for you both.

Love,
T. K.

December 19ᵗʰ, 2009

We are all scared we are going to loose you. It's okay to be scared. We are still here for you and the family no matter how the battle goes. We will all look to God to help us through this. Did you know that *God* spelled backward is *dog*? Better give Poko an extra hug just in case. Hugs to you and Mickie.

D. O.

December 28ᵗʰ, 2009

Hey Ken, I was just browsing through YouTube this weekend and stumbled across a video that made me think of you. It is quite lengthy; however, I think it is certainly worth watching and is something I think you can relate to. It certainly reminds me a lot of you.

This is a video of Carnegie Mellon Professor, Randy Pausch's last lecture. He was diagnosed with the beast and gave a very motivational last talk. I could sit here and explain it, but watching it will do it justice. I hope you have the opportunity to watch this in its entirety: http://www.youtube.com/watch?=ji5_MqicxSo.

God bless you, Ken. We love you.

J. H.

December 30th, 2009

Hi Mr. Kelly! It's C.D., A. gets your journal updates through email, so I use her log-in to check up on you for myself. I love your enthusiasm today! Many healing prayers coming your way!

A. K.

December 30th, 2009

Dear Ken, I am so excited to hear good news for you. How encouraging is that PSA (prostate-specific antigen)? As for the new game plan, count me in. I'm right beside you all the way. If I can take a minute and just thank you also from the bottom of my heart for Christmas Day dinner. It was such a gift from you and really summed up the true meaning of the day. I give thanks for every day, every moment, every obstacle, every success, every celebration, every friend and every miracle. You, my friend, are getting a miracle! I pray for you. God is merciful.

L. M. Y.

December 30th, 2009

Great news! Be safe out there.

J. W.

December 30th, 2009

Ken, such great news and what an outlook for the new year. S. and I continue to keep you in our prayers. We send you warm hugs and lots of *love*!

R. T.

December 30th, 2009

Great news, Ken.

W. G.

December 30th, 2009

Ken, this is great news. I will pray for you. Keep your head up and keep on smiling. I think about you on a daily basis. Keep in touch.

Love,
K. H.

December 30th, 2009

What awesome news today! I was so excited to hear that your PSA is down and as low as it is. *Wow!* I am sure that having a good game plan is a relief for you too. It empowers me when I feel like I am part of a working plan.

I am honored that you have let me be part of this journey with you, and I am thrilled to celebrate this moment with you.

Love,
A. R.

December 30ᵗʰ, 2009

Dear Ken, I just read your last journal entry. How thankful we all are for your good news! God continues to watch over you and bless you. Thank you for sharing your journey.

Here's to a happy and healthy New Year! Love to you and Mickie.

S. W.

December 30ᵗʰ, 2009

Ken, we are both happy to hear the news. We are here for you anytime you need us, and we are going to pray this for you. We *believe* that God Almighty can heal you. That is what we will continue to keep praying for as you go through this battle. The beast has already been put under the feet of Jesus, and so we will keep standing with you. Praying for the strength and to be comfortable during this season of your life. We love you!

T. and S. K.

December 30ᵗʰ, 2009

You are unbelievable, my dear little cousin! I am enthused! I am ecstatic! I'll do it for you. *Wow, holy* cow! *Yeah!* Now I am going outside to jump! Only the *best* news gets me to jump. Talk about the king of understatement! I am so happy for you, Kenny. Did you figure that out? I love you. Big hugs for you and Mickie too.

J. F. F.

December 30th, 2009

That's great news, Ken! Happy to hear that you are doing better. Happy New Year to you and Mickie.

S. D. and Family

December 31st, 2009

Great news, Ken! A good start for a Happy New Year. God bless.

B. S.

January 1st, 2010

Happy New Year and congratulations on the great news. God is good! It is obvious that you still have much to teach the rest of us!

C. C.

January 4th, 2010

Happy New Year, Ken! Whatever you do, don't give up and know that we're all here. Some close and some far away but you are never far from our thoughts and prayers!

K. N. B.

January 7th, 2010

Ken, just praying for you today. Just wanted to say hello and say I hope your day is well. Hoping the beast stays quiet for you this New Year.

Love,
T. and S. K.

January 11ᵗʰ, 2010

I just read your newest journal entry. Words cannot express how sad I am that you have to endure such pain. You are such a kind and gentle man. I pray that your faith remains strong throughout this test that you have been given. You are forever in my prayers.

S. W.

January 11ᵗʰ, 2010

I am sorry to hear that you had a hard couple of days. Your battle is a hard one and I know the chemicals make it hard too. I am glad to hear that the side effects have subsided. You are a strong man and I will continue to pray for you.

Love,
A. R.

January 11ᵗʰ, 2010

Every time you get back up, you knock the beast back down. Keep the beast in its place. Be safe, stay warm and eat cookies.

J. W.

January 11ᵗʰ, 2010

Always here for you, Mr. Kelly.

L. L.

January 11ᵗʰ, 2010

Ken, S. and I continue to pray for you and Mickie. We are more than willing to be there for you on your "not-so-good days" and will continue to do so. Perhaps through our prayers and support for you both, we might just be able to repay a little of the numerous times you have done the same for us and for all that know and love you.

Love you,
R. and S. T.

January 11ᵗʰ, 2010

Ken, as many have told you, you are strong and have done well. We are all amazed how you have come back and, at times even stronger. You truly amaze me. There are many that would just lie down and let the beast win and we are so very happy you have not. We are all praying for you to keep up the good fight. We are all here for you whenever you need any of us. God bless you and Mickie.

T. K.

January 11ᵗʰ, 2010

Ken, I love what you wrote about Confucius. It really is not about falling, but about the desire to keep going. Your strength gives all of us inspiration and I hope we can give this support back to you. Keep the faith.

I have a close friend with lymphoma and brain cancer and he has fought the beast for over three years. It can be done and he is the proof. God bless.

B. S.

January 11ᵗʰ, 2010

Uncle Ken, I am glad to hear you are feeling better after this last battle with the beast. I have always heard that in order to defeat your "beast" (whatever it may be), you need to learn the most you can about them. I'm thinking your beast hasn't heard that rule and hasn't taken the time to get to know you and see all the support behind you. If the beast had done his or her (I don't want to be discriminatory!) homework, the "beast" would know it didn't stand a chance when they entered this battle! I will continue to pray for you and for that "shot"!

Love,
A. B.

January 11ᵗʰ, 2010

Ken, the angel in your pocket is working! Tough times do not last forever, but tough people do. Keep squeezing the angel.

T. C.

January 11ᵗʰ, 2010

You always have and always will make me proud. I cannot explain what a true inspiration you are. Thanks and my thoughts and hopes are with you.

D. E.

January 11ᵗʰ, 2010

You are inspiration! You help us to refocus on the things that "really" matter! Thank you!

L. O.

January 11ᵗʰ, 2010

You are an inspiration to many! God bless! Glad you are feeling better!

S. D.

January 12th, 2010

Ken, I think about you and your fight against the beast daily. I pray for you daily. Funny thing, whether you up or down, you always seem to bring a smile to my face. Bless you for the man you are.

K. G.

January 12th, 2010

You have been in my heart and on my mind the last few days. So glad the first onslaught is now history. Love you!

J. F. F.

January 13th, 2010

Ken, that's a wonderful quote to live by! "*Our greatest glory is not in never falling but in rising every time we fall*".

Keep on fighting and we'll be fighting with you in positive thoughts and many payers for you!

K. N. B.

January 19th, 2010

Hey Ken, knowing you for as long as I have known you, the beast may knock you down; but I know that you will rise. If you need help getting up, you know that all you have to do is give me a call and I will be there 24-7.

K. and I send our love to you and Mickie. God bless you and give you the strength that you need to beat this thing.

P. H.

January 28th, 2010

Dear Ken, reading this last journal entry takes my breath away. Ever the teacher! You and Mickie are in my prayers. J. and I send our love.

S. W.

January 28th, 2010

What is there to say to you, my friend, except that we continue to keep you in our prayers, our thoughts; and of course, we send you our love always.

S. and R. T.

January 29th, 2010

One hundred forty-one days until the cruise, and that's all I have to say about that.

D. O.

January 29th, 2010

Thanks for the reminder. Peace!

C. C.

January 30th, 2010

Ken, you are the strongest person that I have ever met! Your words of wisdom and hope are incredible! I pray every day for you and then you write words to lift all of us up!

Everyone should step back sometimes and remember that no matter how steep the mountain, my good friend, Ken Kelly, says,

"*You can climb it*"! Words to live by! Tell Mickie we send our love from Steuben County and you just beat this thing! I have faith that you will!

A. B.

February 4th, 2010

Ken, I am sorry for your continuing struggles. I pray that you will continue to find the courage to fight. My heart still aches to know that you are going through all of this. You and Poko are in my thoughts.

Love, C. B.

February 4th, 2010

Dearest Ken, your brother and I pray each and every day for you, and you are always, every minute of every day, in our thoughts. Please remain strong as you have been. We love you and are with you always. We are here for you at all times, day or night.

Love, E. and K. K.

February 4th, 2010

Ken, there is no need to apologize for your crying or your asking. I suspect Jesus asked the same thing and cried too. We who love you, care about you, and pray for you will always be there for you. Love you, Ken.

R. T.

February 4th, 2010

You are always in my prayers, but today I will add an extra one up for you. The Lord will provide you the strength and peace as needed, and He is capable of all that we ask.

C. C.

February 4th, 2010

Ken, I am so sorry you and Poko are so sad. Know we are all praying for you and are standing with you at all times. Hope your chemo went well today. Rest this weekend and call if you need anything.

Love,
T. and S. K.

February 4th, 2010

Mr. Kelly, thank you for sharing with us all. We will always be with you! *Thank you* for being in our lives. Hugs and prayers are always with you.

D. R. and B. C.

February 4th, 2010

Uncle Ken, sometimes I have no words. I just love you so much. You are always on my heart and on my mind. I pray the side effects will be minimal and you will be filled with the warmth of our love.

Love,
A. R.

February 4ᵗʰ, 2010

Uncle Ken, ditto what A. said. We are praying with you, for you and for everyone else going through this. I hope you find some peace and some laughter during this treatment so it doesn't seem so bad.

We are here for you and we love you.

R., A., A. and T. B.

February 4ᵗʰ, 2010

You are in my thoughts and prayers.

B. H.

February 4ᵗʰ, 2010

Dear Ken, my heart hurts for you today. Stay strong in your faith, He is with you always.

Love, The W.'s S. W.

February 4ᵗʰ, 2010

I pray every day that the beast takes no more of my friends. I know that you are a very strong person. I firmly believe that God never gives us more that we can handle. I pray that one day, they will find a cure for the beast. You are always in my prayers, my friend.

M. B.

February 4ᵗʰ, 2010

I am sending you lots of love. We don't have any guarantees, any of us, but when we face such direct feedback from the universe, it is hard to ignore. You certainly got a clear message. I am sorry for this pain that comes with this chemo and I am sorry that Poko is going downhill too. I also admire your courage and your ability to look fear in the face. You raise the resonance of the world with your courage.

I love you,
J. F. F.

February 5th, 2010

I pray for you daily. I believe He is listening. God is great and will give you all the strength you need.

K. G.

February 7th, 2010

Ken, thank you for providing us with these updates. I can't tell you how much they mean to me and everybody else. I find it easier knowing how you are feeling. I look forward to my time at work with you. I think the laughter that we all share far outweighs the frustrating times that we endure. For twelve years now I have been able to call you family. I am never afraid to come to you. While there used to be times I was afraid, the years have made it much easier. You inspire me as you do everybody else.

You have taught me to never give up. I will never forget how much support I was given when my dad passed away. While it was one of the most painful times of my life, you let me know it would all be okay. It didn't take words, I just knew.

Thank you, Ken, for the person you are. We all love you and care for you. You are our inspiration.

L. C.

February 7th, 2010

I know that I have not been in touch like I should. I am sorry. I have seen this road, and it is a hard one. I hope that I can give you any support that you could want. It makes me feel small, worrying about all the little problems I face. I hope you have the best day ever today and tomorrow.

D. K.

February 7th, 2010

Ken, I was grateful to hear the docs were able to provide you with meds to tame the side effects. As a friend, who is far away, I appreciate your updates in this journal. I came home from service this morning and had to see if you had checked in to let us all know how the beast was behaving this weekend. I was relieved to hear that your spirits were up.

Your writing reminded me of a verse that our pastor recently preached a sermon on: "*Therefore, since we have been justified through faith, we have peace with God through our Lord Jesus Christ, through whom we have gained access by faith into this grace in which we now stand. And we rejoice in the hope of glory of God. Not only so, but we also rejoice in our sufferings, because we know that suffering produces perseverance; perseverance, character, and character, hope. And hope does not disappoint us because God has poured out His love into our hearts by the Holy Spirit, whom He has given us*" (Romans 5:1–5).

Thank you for sharing your happiness and your pain. Sharing the burden helps each of us.

C. C.

February 7th, 2010

Our dad's both showed us we have no guarantees on tomorrow. None of us do. It's all about embracing this moment. God bless you,

Kenny. You are so rich. I am also glad you are feeling so much better. Love you.

J. F. F.

February 7th, 2010

"I hope that they will only remember the dash between the dates."
Ken, this was one of the most powerful and thought-provoking statements I have read during your blogging. Somehow, I don't think they could put enough dashes between your dates to represent what you have meant to individuals and communities alike. I'm glad to hear you have found some comfort again from side effects. Be safe.

J. W.

February 7th, 2010

Ken, your last journal entry made me tear up at the thought of you giving in. You have every right to be angry and fearful, but we're here with you. I always remember you to be a man of medicine, willing to do anything and go to any length to help a patient. After reading this recent entry, it fills my heart with cheer and brings a smile to my face knowing you're on the move again. You can see the happiness in each day. Keep going, Ken! It has been said probably a million times, but *we are here* both close and far away!

K. N. B.

February 8th, 2010

Ken, your strength through this beast has shown me we can go through anything if we have the faith, the friends and the family that you have to support you. I always know how family and friends must look to you, but now I see how important it is to have them and to be able to talk and have their support. After reading all the entries, I see how the words they write can help you feel loved and not alone. Keep strong and know we are all here for you. We all love you and are praying for you, Mickie and Poko.

Love,
T. and S. K.

February 8th, 2010

Uncle Ken, when the day comes that we have to look at the dash, know that your dash will be double bolded.

You have inspired, changed and made a difference in so many lives through your teachings, perseverance and love. The privileged "few" that are able to share this story with you through this medium are truly a testament to that fact. Because of that, I am confident there are many more lives out there that you have changed for the better. They have been unable to express that to you, but have "paid your efforts forward". Know in your heart that you truly have made a difference, for the better, in many lives of mankind.

I am happy to hear the extra meds, given to ward off the side effects, worked for you and you were able to find some relief in this battle. I pray that your battles with this beast keep you out in front.

I love, you,
A. B.

February 9th, 2010

Hi Kenny, sorry it took me until tonight to catch up on your journal. I do hope you are feeling better as this comes to you. You are always in my thoughts and prayers.

You are an incredible gift, teacher and reminder to us all about how limited our time on earth is. A reminder about the most important thing in life is love and sharing it with others. I'm sorry you have to take this difficult journey. I know God knows what an incredible teacher you are and, in His infinite wisdom, has brought us all back together through your journey. I know that He knows that you are the "rock," the "strength" and the "reminder" to us all. Thank you for being you. You are a gift to us all who love and care about you. I'm praying too for the find of a cure for this beast within. You don't deserve pain and illness, but God knows. He knows how special you are and always have been to so many. You are strong and I pray for a cure and for the painful beast to go away, but also leave us here with you in good health. You deserve the best. You are in my thoughts and prayers.

God bless you.

Love,
K. L. H.

February 9th, 2010

You truly are one of my heroes and I enjoy coming to work, not only for the challenges, but to share a good laugh or smile with my boss in the morning from time to time. Your words are inspirational and you continue to teach us all. Stay strong, Ken.

B. J.O.

February 23rd, 2010

In honor of Ken Kelly, my teacher and my friend.

D. E.

February 23rd, 2010

That is great news to hear and I am so happy for you. I will keep you in my prayers and hope it keeps getting better from here. Have a great day.

M. B.

February 23rd, 2010

Dear Ken, I just read your latest journal entry. It was like a breath of fresh air! God is truly watching over you. I can't express how happy I am for both you and Mickie. I will continue to keep you in my prayers.

S. W.

February 23rd, 2010

I just read your journal entry today and that is outstanding news! I am so glad to hear that you are doing so well. Stay strong, my good friend! Keep up the good work!

K. T.

February 23rd, 2010

This is great news! Jumping for joy with this good report! Praying for complete healing.

T. H.

February 23rd, 2010

Ken, we praise Jesus for this report! We all will continue to pray for you throughout this thing with the beast for however long it takes. As for J., I think the very same thing, jump small but jump for joy. The Lord is in control of your life, not that beast. Love you and we are jumping for you!

T. K.

February 23rd, 2010

Yeah, that is amazing news. Prayers are still with you! Stay strong.

J. B.

February 23rd, 2010

This is great news, Ken!

J. M.

February 23rd, 2010

Woohooo! Rejoicing with you, Ken!

J. D.

February 23rd, 2010

Ken, if you walk "fastly" outside, stand still and listen very carefully—ear to the northwest and eyes closed—you can hear me praising God for the good news! You can also hear the dogs barking and telling me to shut up! Uh-oh, here come the cops now! LOL Praise God! Oh, miss you. Come visit here.

Love,
D. T.

February 23, 2010

Ken, great news is always welcome, and your great news is even more welcome because it is something we have all been waiting to hear. It's indeed what we have all been hoping and praying for. The key now is to keep these thoughts and prayers. J. also sends her congratulations. We will continue to pray for your well being and progress.

Love you,
J. H. and J. V.

February 23rd, 2010

Anything is possible for a man with great inner strength, courage and faith. So happy to hear this news. Prayers can move mountains! Your friends will continue to pray for the continuation of this great news.

Our love always,
S. and R. T.

February 23rd, 2010

Yippeee!

R. M.

February 23rd, 2010

What great news, Kenny! Keep up the good work! Remember not to push yourself. Save your energy to get healthier and healthier!

Love,
L. B.

February 23rd, 2010

Uncle Ken, what *awesome* news! So happy for you and Mickie! We love you!

A. B.

February 23rd, 2010

I will continue to pray every day for even better news. I want to jump for joy myself. Just take it one day at a time and keep going with it.

M. B.

February 23rd, 2010

I will go jump for you! Yeah! I understand your caution, but this is really the most exuberant I have ever heard you! I am so glad the pain is down. That is a miracle! Still *yeah*! I love you!

J. F. F.

February 23rd, 2010

Ken, our prayers are being answered and I hope they continue. I am so happy for you that I cannot express it in words. I will continue to pray for you. I am definitely rejoicing with you. I hope the good news continues and brings you happiness each and every day.

E. Z. (Y.)

February 24th, 2010

Ditto to all the other posts as prayers are being answered! We will keep praying!

C. C.

February 25th, 2010

Ken and Mickie, this is the best news that we have heard in a long time. I am still praying for you. I knew you could do it. We come from strong stock and I am pleased to hear the good news. When A. called, she was ecstatic. She sure thinks the world of her Uncle Ken and Aunt Mickie.

All my blessings,
J. L.

February 28ᵗʰ, 2010

This is great to hear, Ken. May God bless.

B. H.

February 28ᵗʰ, 2010

All good news, you are looking great! Looking forward to more good news.

J. D.

March 1ˢᵗ, 2010

All I can say is yeah! Awesome to see you feeling better.

D. O.

March 5ᵗʰ, 2010

Ken, I get so blessed when I read your journal, whether it is sad news or happy news. You are encouraging people when you write and the way your live your life. I know even when you are at home, all alone, you get scared and feel alone; but you are always so upbeat when anyone shows up to your house. You have really done great to try to be up no matter what is going on inside and that makes us so proud to know you. I pray for you daily and we will continue until this battle is over. Your family and friends are always here for you.

Thank you for keeping us in the loop, whether it is good or bad. The sunshine will always make you better, but it is still too cold for you to run around in a tank top. You have to wait until at least the snow melts before I can catch you out on the porch sunning yourself.

T. K.

March 5ᵗʰ, 2010

It is good to hear that you are feeling better today after your treatment. I do know what it is like to be inspired by someone or something that someone has written or said. You have inspired me! I am in awe of your strength. When you have been talking about what is important to you, friends and family, it makes me realize that I should embrace all those moments. We will continue to travel this journey with you, good and bad moments. Have a wonderful *sunny* weekend!

Love,
A. R.

March 5ᵗʰ, 2010

We, my dear Ken, take our inspiration from you!

R. T.

March 5ᵗʰ, 2010

Uncle Ken, I believe that what you learn and pass on *absolutely* counts. I wouldn't call you an imitator but rather a scholar. Whether you learn by experience or gain your knowledge through observing, listening and/or reading, the fact is that you have absorbed this into your personal life. You choose to live by these teachings and this makes you a teacher and a good example for all those around you.

Keep reading and absorbing because we are still listening and learning.

A. B.

March 5ᵗʰ, 2010

Just being able to call you my friend means so much to me. You inspire me more than you can imagine. I asked for your advice a while back and I am going to do exactly as you advised. Even though it scares me, I believe that is going to help. You are a very great person, my friend.

M. B.

March 7ᵗʰ, 2010

Awesome!

D. O.

March 15ᵗʰ, 2010

Ken, that's what the doctors get paid for—to listen! If you are in pain, then they need to hear it. You are not whining by any means. By the way, try to enjoy yourself St. Patty's Day. Love you.

M. K.

March 15ᵗʰ, 2010

Ken, I know that the pains come with the beast, but when praying for you, I had a thought. Do what you may, but maybe you need a better mattress for more support. I know yours is fairly new, but it may not be good for your back. Maybe you should spend a night trying out different kinds, and see if they feel better.

Dear precious Jesus, guide Ken in the direction he should go. Dear Jesus, relieve this pain from him.

T. K.

March 15th, 2010

Uncle Ken, you shouldn't feel like you are bothering the doctors. That is their job to help you, and I know that your oncologist is fighting for you too. He wants you to be comfortable. He is a great doctor and he will understand what you are going through. We all know that you aren't a whiner, quite the opposite.

Could it be the motorcycle rides that are causing you the discomfort? You have a heavy bike, and the way you have to sit on it may not help with any pain you are feeling.

We will continue to pray for you and this pain that has resurfaced. Please call the doctor, and if they can help, let them do what they can.

Love always,
A. R.

March 15th, 2010

Ken, you are not a whiner by any stretch of the imagination. Call your doctor, and see what he has to say. After all, isn't that what they get paid for? I'm quite sure that he will not feel that you are bothering him. Please make the call. We pray for you every day.

M. B.

March 15th, 2010

Oh Kenny, how discouraging. Still, talk to the doctor, honey. I sure understand feelings though. I am doing better too and have a good prognosis. That is, if I do what I am told, like sitting still for several weeks while taking pills. *Me?* Yup, sometimes we have to go ask for help. I hope you have some relief by now. I am so sorry the pain has increased. It is scary. I love you. Thinking of you, my dearest cousin.

J. F. F.

March 16th, 2010

At a loss for words, Ken. I am pretty darn sure you are anything else but a whiner. You are *strong* and you can beat the beast. Keep believing. Keep your faith. Prayers are with you.

Love you.

R. T.

March 16th, 2010

Some pain, yes. Pain that ruins your day, no! Maybe a trip to a pain clinic would be beneficial? There are alternative treatments to try that may alleviate your discomfort without pharmaceutical fogging. As an added bonus, you wouldn't feel as though you were whining (even though you aren't) because that is what they are there for. If you are up for the trip, Roswell has an amazing pain clinic.

Hoping for relief for you.

J. W.

March 16th, 2010

I am sending you the biggest hug as I write this. If I can get away from sitting with C. tonight, I will be over to give you that hug in person, also bring you your favorite beer.

D. O.

March 16th, 2010

Ken, you are truly one of the strongest men I know. You bring hope to those who believe that all is lost. Your perseverance is amazing. You will get ahead of the beast. You are in mine and L.'s prayers. If there is anything we can do, please feel free to get ahold of me.

B. C.

March 16th, 2010

Mr. Kelly, my prayers and thoughts are with you and your family right now through this tough time. I hope you feel better soon.

L. L.

March 16th, 2010

Hug!

J. W.

March 16th, 2010

I know we just talked on the phone; however, I want you to know that I would drive right over to Canandaigua, give you a hug and anything else I have to give that would make your day a little brighter. I would also bring some beer too!

R. T.

March 16th, 2010

I am hugging you and praying with you. You will get back in front of the beast. I think about how you are doing every day and know that you will get stronger.

M. B.

March 16th, 2010

Dear Ken, I am sending you hugs galore and lots of prayers.

S. W.

March 16th, 2010

Ken, I hope you can feel my hug! I'm praying for you right now. Thank you for continuing to be an inspiration in spite of your struggles.

L. O.

March 16th, 2010

Hugs! Hugs and prayers going out for you!

C. C.

March 16th, 2010

Well, that is bad news but also good news. At least there is something to alleviate the pain and a treatment to push back with. I am sorry for the additional pain, Kenny, but glad your doctor is on top of it. He sounds like a good man and very responsive to your needs. I am sending you a big hug and lots of love.

J. F. F.

March 17ᵗʰ, 2010

Ken, I'm sorry to hear this, but stay strong. You are a fighter. Here are three hugs. One from myself, one from D. and one from M. We are praying for you!

J. B.

March 17ᵗʰ, 2010

Sending hugs your way.

L. C.

March 17ᵗʰ, 2010

Ken, my thoughts, prayers and hugs are with you. I hope this beast will leave you and at least leave you comfortable.

J. L.

March 20ᵗʰ, 2010

The biggest hug in the world for my Uncle Ken!

Love,
D. and L. M. Y.

March 23ʳᵈ, 2010

I am praying so hard for you today. Praying that God will take the pain away and give you the strength you need to walk through this. You are surrounded by people who love you immensely and will do anything and everything to walk beside you, carry you, hold you, comfort you, laugh with you and cry with you. Just know you aren't alone.

Love, XO,
A. R.

March 23ʳᵈ, 2010

We are all here for you. Sending you hugs and prayers.

Love,
T. and S. K.

March 26ᵗʰ, 2010

Hi Ken, greetings from Wisconsin. B. and I are praying for you and Mickie. You are the best boss I ever had. Thank you for sharing your story so openly. It reminds me of what things are truly important and what is just static.

You said you needed a hug, so sending one your way.

P. F.

March 28ᵗʰ, 2010

Ken, you are loved and prayed for.

R. T.

March 28ᵗʰ, 2010

You, my friend, would never let anyone down knowingly or unknowingly. You are a very strong person and you will beat this beast within you. Our prayers are with you every day. You will get stronger and you will survive this, my friend.

M. B.

March 28ᵗʰ, 2010

Even though I live far away, I fight the beast with you. You are not alone in your battle. There are many all across the country picking up the sword and swinging it on your behalf. Washington kisses, hugs and prayers.

D. T.

March 28ᵗʰ, 2010

I think you are remarkable in your abilities to manage both your business and personal affairs despite the challenges thrown at you. Giving yourself the time you need to deal with this hurdle by trusting in the team you have in place reinforces your confidence in them. Sending positive thoughts your way.

J. W.

March 28ᵗʰ, 2010

Dearest Ken, I am so saddened that you continue to suffer with this wretched beast. I pray that God continues to give you and Mickie the strength you need to get through each day. You are such a kind and gentle soul. You are forever in my prayers.

S. W.

March 28th, 2010

I wish you luck on Monday, Kenny. Also thinking of Mickie and your family. I love you.

L. B.

March 28th, 2010

Ken, K. and I are hoping that your CT (computed tomography) scan this week will flush the beast into the open. Then the doctors can give you some relief from your discomfort.

You, Sir, have put together a fantastic organization that will pick you up and will never be let down by you. The technicians, the management, the billing staff and all that work at Finger Lakes Ambulance are your friends and family. They are highly dedicated and professional. That is because you have demanded no less.

Here are prayers for you and Mickie, that God may comfort you during this new challenge.

P. H.

March 28th, 2010

We *can't* fail, Kenny. Kumbaya, my Lord, kumbaya.

J. F. F.

March 28th, 2010

I am thinking about you and your fight. I will pray that the four weeks go by fast and with a good outcome.

J. D.

March 28ᵗʰ, 2010

We are all with you and love you. Big hugs from L. and I.

D. O.

March 28ᵗʰ, 2010

Ken, all the best this week with tests and treatment. Our thoughts will be with you.

J. and T. D.

March 29ᵗʰ, 2010

Ken, we are praying for you. Praying that all the tests will direct the doctors to treat every part of this beast. As I have told you before, I wish I could be one quarter as strong as you have been throughout this battle. You have encouraged so many people. Keep strong and trust Jesus. He is in control of your life, not the beast. Hugs to you and Mickie. We love you both.

T. K.

March 29ᵗʰ, 2010

Ken, I'm with you wherever you go. I'm with you whatever you need.

Love,
L. M. Y.

March 29ᵗʰ, 2010

Mr. Kelly, you have been here for all of us for so long and have taught us all so much every day! Just know that good days and bad days, we, your friends and employees, will be here. So the days when work seems to be too big of a task or when focus just isn't in the cards, know we are here. There is no way to say thank you for the things you have taught us and done for us other than to stand up when you need us.

Thank you for being our leader in so many ways!

S. S.

March 29th, 2010

Ken-Ken, thinking of you and hoping for you. You are an inspiration and a warrior. As you continue to lead the troops, don't forget to take care of the Colonel.

The very best of luck today and in the future.

C. T. (#246)

March 29th, 2010

Still praying and sending much love to you.

J. B.

March 29th, 2010

Hi, Kenny. Boy, you have been up and down and all around these past few weeks with this awful beast. You are in my thoughts and prayers. I pray that the beast is caught along with all its nasty clones. God bless you, Ken. You truly are an inspiration to everyone who loves and cares about you.

Many loving thoughts and prayers coming your way for healing, sleep when you want it, no more pain and everything that brings you joy.

Love,
K. L. H.

March 29ᵗʰ, 2010

Ken, my thoughts and prayers are with you every day. Hang in there!

J. L.

March 30ᵗʰ, 2010

Good morning, Ken. Yet again your words inspire me. As I was reading them, I was listening to an album of compositions by Sir William Walton. The album is called *English Coral Music*. My favorite, which I was listening to, is "Missa Brevis" (containing the movements of Kyrie, Santus and Benedicuts), "Angus Dei" and "Gloria." This music, which I discovered yesterday, brings me peace and, in my thoughts, quite close to God. I recommend it if you haven't already heard it. I find it best to listen to when deep in thought or while driving. Much like your words today, it is helping me to focus on the good and peace in the world and to banish hate.

May God bless you and your family. We are all with you on this journey. Thank you for everything.

With love,
J. H.

March 30ᵗʰ, 2010

Good morning, Ken. Your words are opening up my eyes to life, how to take it on and how to deal with everything that we walk through in life. I have to agree with you about what God has waiting for us on the other side.

I hope you are feeling good today and you are in my prayers. Have a great day, Sir.

Your friend,
M. B.

March 30th, 2010

Ken, your outlook is a goal that we should all strive for. As we enter Holy Week, we will pray for you, Ken, that God keeps you strong and comforts you, Mickie and all your family. Have a nice Easter.

P. H.

March 30th, 2010

Ken Kelly, *you rock*! You are one in a million. I believe that God sends angels to us for whatever reason. I believe that you are one of God's angels.

Wishing you and Mickie a most blessed Easter.

Love,
S. and J. W.

March 30th, 2010

Good afternoon, Ken. I truly thank you for your most recent post. I have learned a great deal from you. F. and I will say a little prayer for you and Mickie during the Easter holiday. I hope with the warm weather coming, you can pull the bike out and go enjoy a terrific ride. I always found a certain piece of spirituality riding on a long country road. I hope your pain is minimal and you continue to find the comfort surrounding you.

All our love,
F. and B. J. O.
(And the Stu Dog, 'cause he rocks like Poko)

March 30th, 2010

In the true spirit of Ken Kelly, you continue teaching by sharing your thoughts and feelings, when all others would have given up. Thank you, Ken, for everything.

C. T.

March 30th, 2010

You were an inspiration and role model to me when I was fifteen years old, as a punk kid working in a grocery store. Now I am rapidly closing in on forty, have a wife, two kids, a great career; and yet you continue to inspire me and truly be someone I look up to.

Thank you, Ken, for being a true friend, a role model and an inspiration. Stay strong, my brother. You are thought of often.

Love ya,
K. T.

March 30th, 2010

Ken, I agree with P. I will keep you, Mickie, Poko, family and all the medical staff in my prayers and thoughts. Your outlook is positive and it's something everyone should strive for. You're helping others, Ken, just like you wanted to do in this life when you got into medicine.

Keep going, Ken. We're all here for you and praying for you to have the strength you need.

K. N. B.

March 30ᵗʰ, 2010

No words to say, except very well put and as always. You are still teaching all of us even as you fight. Never change. All our love and prayers coming your way!

J. B.

March 30ᵗʰ, 2010

Ken, once again your thoughts are an inspiration. I know when you are having a bad day and that always bothers me. I also know when you are having a better day. I pray you have many better ones. Reading your entry, the words almost took on a glow, or is that the radiation you are having? I see you laughing, so I've completed my task.

Love, D. O.

March 30ᵗʰ, 2010

Ken, over the years you were my mentor. You got me into my first EMT class in Canandaigua. You were my crew chief, bowling buddy and my dearest friend. To this day you are still teaching me things that really matter. I will never forget what you have taught me. The stories that we could share are forever in my thoughts. Your mom dispatching for Canandaigua and losing her teeth, A. bringing your mother to the base in his camouflaged car—these are just a few memories. You are like a big brother to me and as I always say, family sticks together. So I am there for you, in thoughts and prayers. Love you and Mickie for being so kind to others.

Love,
K. H.

March 30th, 2010

A small token of appreciation for the wealth of wisdom you share with us all. We thank you.

Anonymous

April 2nd, 2010

Ken, here is a link to a truly inspirational story: http://ww.examiner.com/x-1029-Pet-News-Examiner-y2010m4d2Whale-tags-along-surfers-marathon-paddle-for-breast-cancer-Photo. This is God's work at its best. He shows us that He walks with us and that He is great. Nature and human become one for the cause of cancer research. When I saw this, I immediately thought of you, your faith and your love for the outdoors, especially the ocean.

May God bless you and your family at this most Holy weekend.

J. H.

April 5th, 2010

Ken, I enjoy your writings so much. Don't quit. I wish you peace and good night's rest, my man.

J. K.

April 7ᵗʰ, 2010

Ken, you had a huge impact on my life as well as countless others. In fact, you still impact my life every day. I will never forget "a bradycardic kid is a hypoxic kid". I strive to be like you and other paramedics that I respect. You know what my dad was told, not once but twice, and he is still in remission. So don't ever give up hope. Know that there are millions and probable trillions of prayers out there for you. Miss you and thank you. *Hugs!*

T. W. D.

April 19ᵗʰ, 2010

"He ain't heavy, he's my brother." We are here for you now and will be for as long as it takes to beat the beast.

R. T.

April 19ᵗʰ, 2010

Hey Ken, just letting you know that I am thinking of you and continue to pray for you. You have been, and continue to be, an inspiration to many. Know that we, who have been inspired, are here for you.

J. D.

April 19ᵗʰ, 2010

Hi, Ken, having worked with cancer patients, I have met many strong and caring people. You are among the strongest I have known. B. and I have you in our thoughts and prayers. Your openness as you fight this beast is amazing and inspiring. I thank you for sharing this with so many.

P. F.

April 19th, 2010

Dear Ken, you've been unbelievably strong for so long, take some downtime. All the people who love you and care about you have your back! Always in my thoughts and prayers.

S. W.

April 19th, 2010

Ken, seeing what you and Mickie are going through has saddened me, so I cry for you both often. As I've been praying for you both, I get the sense that, through Jesus, you will be strong. It says that, through your weakness, He will make you strong. I have no idea what that means for you two, but that is the verse I have been getting this past week for you both. We are here to carry you, just as Jesus does each day. Even if it is only a quick, "Hello, how are you?" we are thinking and praying for you and Mickie always.

Love,
T. K.

April 19th, 2010

We will, we will rock the beast! My, oh my, what a wonderful day headed your way! *Hugs!*

D. R.

April 19th, 2010

Mr. Kelly, you have been so strong in your fight against the beast. It is okay to have a bad day and to reach out to all to give you strength.

I hope that you can find some healing in this prayer that is said every week in my temple. It seems most appropriate now since it is also for the spirit that today seems to be what is most needed.

Mi Shebeirach, Mi Shebeirach.

L. R. T.

April 19th, 2010

Ken, I hope your day has become a bit easier. I recommend sitting outside and watching the beautiful sunset. You are one of the strongest men I know. Hang in there. Cookies await you at the end of this recent hill. Love you and Mickie always.

F. and B. J.O

April 19th, 2010

You, my friend, are allowed to have a moment of weakness; and I know that it is only for a moment. You are one of the most caring and giving people that I know. D. and I need to get out to see you, but it will have to wait until after this week is over. Yes, my friend, I took your advice; and I am having the surgery. We will be out afterward. In the meantime, you stay strong and know that our prayers are with you always.

M. B.

April 19ᵗʰ, 2010

Ken, you are certainly allowed a moment of weakness. You are human and you can do this.

Cancer is so limited. It cannot cripple love. It cannot shatter hope. It cannot corrode faith. It cannot eat away peace. It cannot destroy confidence. It cannot kill friendships. It cannot shut our memories. It cannot silence courage. It cannot reduce eternal life. It cannot quench the spirit.

K. N. B.

April 29ᵗʰ, 2010

On your particularly nauseous days, only put things in your mouth that you won't mind tasting a second time, just in case. Any woman will tell you that chocolate is always a good choice. Thinking of you.

J. W.

April 20ᵗʰ, 2010

Ken, I am so sorry that you are going through this tough time. My prayers are constant, and I am thinking of you and Mickie all the time. May the Lord give you peace and less pain as you continue on this journey.

Love,
J. L.

April 20ᵗʰ, 2010

Uncle Ken, you are a pillar of strength even in your down or weak moments. I hope and pray the side effects that you are experiencing come to an end soon. We are all thinking of you, praying for you, supporting you and are here for you in both your down and up moments. We love you!

A., R., A. and T. B.

April 20ᵗʰ, 2010

Ken, I am sorry so much time has elapsed since we last touched base. In some ways, it seems as if it were only yesterday that we were hoisting a cold one at the Ale House or cutting cases out in the cold.

I was inspired by your words as you have chronicled your journey with what you euphemistically call the "beast". The courage that I admired in you years ago has obviously stayed with you all this time.

You should know that your days as a teacher began long before your time in the paramedical education. Many of the rules one should live by, such as integrity, hard work and decency, I did not glean from any class or textbook. I gleaned it by the example that you set and the challenges that you put in front of me during our days back at Star. For those lessons and the great times we had, I will be eternally grateful.

I sincerely hope for you all the very best and my prayers are with you as you battle this terrible illness.

Your journal has confirmed that procrastination does not do anyone any good and that life should be seized and cherished, for even the small moments add some complexion to the journey.

I plan to stay in touch and am hopeful that N. and I will be in the Upstate soon to pay you a visit. (Hopefully, that thought does not keep you awake at night.) Take care, Ken.

Your friend always,
D. S.

April 20th, 2010

You called me an angel. Now there's a laugh. Picture me with wings and a bottle of Jack. There, I made you smile! See you in the morning.

D. O.

April 22nd, 2010

Ken, you are a loved and adored man. Take a minute and close your eyes. Picture a big cruise ship out on the ocean. It's eighty-five degrees with nothing but sunshine and blue skies. Surround yourself by people who are sharing the same adventure. June 19th, baby! Now if that doesn't lift your spirits, let me know and I'll see what I can do.

We love you,
L., J. and D. Y.

April 29th, 2010

Amen, Ken! Your last entry was simply inspiring. I think we all take it for granted that people are with us until they aren't. We feel so helpless because there are things that should have been resolved prior to that day they left this world. Everyone should take the words that you just spoke of and make the best out of the situations that they are in. I truly believe that it's a blessing to hear these words come from you. God bless you and your family.

B. C.

April 29th, 2010

"Life is way too short, so cherish every second with no regrets" is my new motto on life. Always be true to yourself and your loved ones, and life will go much smoother. Keep your head up and remember that everyone is praying for you.

J. B.

April 29*th*, 2010

Life as we know it may be final. We are all on that journey and yet there is the promise of life everlasting. We have all lost loved ones in this life and yet they are still with us. Their love, understanding and teachings remain and will for countless generations. Those of us that live pass that love, that understanding and those teachings down to our children.

You have not finished your journey. In spite of the difficulties that lay ahead for all of us, we will persevere; and we will persevere together. We are here for you, and together we will seize all the days of our lives.

Love you, Ken.

R. T.

April 29*th*, 2010

Thanks again, for another inspirational message! Thank you for reminding me how significant my life is and how important the people I love are to me. I continue to pray for strength and healing as you battle your "beast".

L. O.

April 29*th*, 2010

Dear Ken, I wanted to share with you how much it means that you are so involved in D.'s life. Even when you are not feeling well, you continue to show you love and devotion for him. He loves you so very much, and it makes his life richer for your being in it. You are such a presence and a force for him. It's in part due to your constant involvement in his world that he is growing up to be such a wonderful young man.

We love you,
L., J. and D. Y.

April 29ᵗʰ, 2010

Wow! We love you!

J. F. F.

April 30ᵗʰ, 2010

Ken, truer words were never written. Advice that we should all heed. DaVinci is credited with, *"Life well spent is long"* and I think that is also true.

Here in the Carolinas, it is my favorite time of year. Beautiful days, comfortable evenings and baseball is in full swing.

Hoping and praying that your downtimes are far surpassed by your uptimes!

D. S.

May 1ˢᵗ, 2010

You are a special part of many lives, and your message was inspirational. Thank you.

Love and hugs,
D. O.

May 15th, 2010

Thank you for the reminder that we all should seize the minute, the hour and the day. However, we are easily strayed to things that in the end mean nothing. Keep us all reminded and again, thank you.

C. C.

May 22nd, 2010

Ken, even when you are alone in the hospital, in your bed or driving your car, remember that you are not alone. You are always in someone's prayers, and the Lord is still holding you in His arms. He will continue until He sees you through the season with the beast.

God bless. So happy you are back home with Mickie.

T. K.

May 22nd, 2010

You have looked *incredibly* better the last few days. The color in your cheeks and lips has returned. Your eyes are bright and clear again and it's good to see.

I'm glad the "tune up" and "oil change" they gave you at Clifton helped get you back on the road again. Be safe.

J. W.

May 22nd, 2010

Hope you will soon be on the mend and enjoying the open air and water on your cruise.

J. D.

May 22ⁿᵈ, 2010

Dear Ken, you are always in our thoughts and in our prayers.

S. and J. W.

May 22ⁿᵈ, 2010

Keeping you in my thoughts and prayers.

B. H.

May 22ⁿᵈ, 2010

Dear Kenny, you are a tower of strength and courage. Thank you for sharing your deepest feelings with us all. You also, by the way, are an incredible writer.

You make all of us who read your journal stop, think, smile, love and smell the roses. All the while waking up to the reality that life is short and letting those around us that we love and care about know that.

I am sorry you have such strong challenges in this lifetime. You certainly have proven over and over the power and depths of your strength and love for, especially your family. You have stepped up to all challenges and faced them with love, knowing and trusting God. You are always in my thoughts and prayers as I continue to be amazed by you and how eloquently you handle these challenges.

God bless you, Kiddo and Mickie too. I hope you have the best cruise ever! There's nothing like a vacation, a cruise to just lie back and soak in the abundance of love in the universe. You continue to inspire, even in your deepest and darkest times.

Here's to warmth, sun, love and energy flowing strongly into you now.

Love,
K. L. H.

May 23rd, 2010

Hi Ken, F. and I ran into B. the other night; and he told us you were able to get out and enjoy some of this good weather on the bike! I'm glad. Please take a nice long ride for me and take in some nice deep breaths on some long country road. I always found that the air seemed to be cleaner and just better when I was cruising along on my bike a little faster than the posted speed limit. Hey, I'm just sayin'!

Enjoy the cruise and create some great memories to bring back and share with your family and friends.

All our love,
F. and B. J. O.

May 24th, 2010

You have a great cruise. The liquid refreshments abound, or so I am told. Keeping you in our prayers. God bless.

R. T.

May 24th, 2010

Have a great trip, relax and try to clear your mind. You deserve it. Thanks for everything over the last few years. I have made some bad choices (O. and the grass thing, LOL). It's funny now, but it wasn't then, so thanks for keeping me. The best choice I ever made was working here. It is a pleasure working for you and Finger Lakes Ambulance. This place is home away from home. Thanks again and have a great time.

A. E.

May 24th, 2010

Hi, Kenny, I hope this week is better. Love you.

J. F. F.

May 26th, 2010

Hey there, Mr. Kelly! I recommend chucky dunking (aka skinny dipping in our younger years) and blueberry wine!

B. B. S.

May 28th, 2010

Hang in there, Ken. Thoughts and prayers are with you, my friend.

D. S.

May 28th, 2010

I read that God always connects us with people for a reason, there are no accidents. I'm so blessed to have been "connected" to you. You certainly have challenged all of us with your thoughts in dealing with your cancer. God bless you, Ken. Stay strong.

S. and J. W.

May 28th, 2010

Memorial Day is a day we remember those that have given their lives in the past and for those that suffer in the battle that is set before them today. Persevere, my friend and brother, because your perseverance to the end, and we all have an end, is what makes you, you! *Semper fi!*

D. T.

May 28th, 2010

Ken and Mickie, I sometimes wonder why I have been cancer free for so long and you have to go through the pain that you do. My thoughts and prayers are with both of you and I hope that this terrible ordeal will be over soon and you can be in remission for a long time.

Love you both,
J. L.

May 28th, 2010

Sounds like another tough one. Thinking of you. Surrender is hard. Love you.

J. F. F.

May 28th, 2010

Ken-Ken, thinking of and hoping for you daily. Wanted to pass along a fond memory. This weekend I took my son, age three, to a race at Limerock Speedway. Thought of you the whole time and kept looking toward the first-aid hut. Be well.

C. T.

May 28th, 2010

I have found that sometimes your greatest fear can turn into your greatest strength. Most people will give into their fear and let it consume them. People like you will channel that fear and turn it into the strength they need to survive whatever obstacle lies before them.

People who have no fear don't feel and are therefore reckless. People who have fear, *feel*! When they channel that fear into survival mode, they tend to be the strongest people we all admire, like you.

God gave us good and evil so we could see the difference and make the right decisions. He also gave us fear and strength. You need to have both to have balance, kind of like oil and vinegar in a salad dressing. With oil and vinegar, alone, on a salad, it's awful and not palatable. But when you mix the two into an emulsion, then add your favorite flavorings (like salt, pepper and other spices), it turns out to be very flavorful and palatable.

The fear and strength you talk about is kind of like *your* salad dressing. When you take the fear you feel and channel it into the strength you portray, you are mixing the emulsion. When you add in all the love and support you feel and that is portrayed from all your family and friends, you are adding the "spices" to make this a palatable or survivable battle against the beast.

When you beat this beast (notice I did not say *if*), you need to market this "Ken Kelly's Own" because it is a winner!

You are *wonderful* even in your down moments because you give so many of us inspiration and are so thought-provoking, to spur us on to be better people. At least for me, that is true.

I wish for this latest round to go easier than the previous. I also wish you a *wonderful* time on your upcoming cruise. I wish I could join you.

All my love,
A. B.

May 28th, 2010

Ken, after reading your latest journal, I thought back to the time when my father was battling his lung cancer. I often thought, *What are they learning from this? Anything new? Would his trials help anyone else? Since his death, is there something the docs learned?* I read

163

you were having the same thoughts. I will continue to pray for you and Mickie that God fills you with faith and trust in Him. These for you and for the docs He has blessed with the knowledge to treat you. If you run out of strength and hope, Ken, borrow it from us! We're learning faith, strength and hope from you. Keep going, Ken!

K. N. B.

May 28th, 2010

Thinking of you.

J. D.

June 3rd, 2010

Hi Kenny. I hope you are feeling better this week. I read your last journal entry about strength, and I would like you to know and understand what I meant when I said, "I admire your strength". I see you as strong because you wake up every morning and try to find something positive to say. Not everyone in this world can do that, healthy or unhealthy. I see your strength when you continue to fight for your life *and* keep working in a position that has impacted the lives of untold numbers of people in this world. The ripple effect of your teaching and your program is unending and will never fade out because it will never reach a shore. For example, my daughter L. is an EMT and working for a YMCA day camp this summer while studying nursing. Our cousin P. L. (J.'s son) is in EMT training. I've got at least two other in-law relatives who are EMTs. Would this profession have borne the responsibility and changes that have come through since you have run your programs? Perhaps. But the fact is that you have put this into action. This doesn't even include the countless citizens lives that have been touched by the hand of *your* grace, Ken.

Please don't confuse your incredible achievements and your ongoing heroic actions with your thoughts that everyone has in their own minds. We all live with fear and self-doubt. It is the strong people who push them aside and carry on with life. Only the strongest of us can take chemo, hop on a motorcycle, go to work another day and still say something positive. All I know is that people who think they don't deserve to be taken care of because they have too much left to do are the people who deserve it most and are the strongest among us.

You are a hero, Kenny. Even when you are alone with your thoughts and fears. Thank you for the gifts you have given all of us through your work, kinship and presence. I will continue looking at you for your whole being, actions, thoughts and deeds. Looking at you as one of the strongest role models I have ever seen. You are truly amazing and always have been.

L. B.

June 3rd, 2010

Dear Ken, because of J., L. and D., I have come to know what a truly wonderful and caring friend you are. That in itself is such a blessing. I hope you know what an inspiration you are to so many. You and Mickie continue to be in my prayers every day.

God bless you,
S. W.

June 3rd, 2010

Ken, I cried when reading your last entry here. It reminds me of what I told my cousin when her son died in a terrible car accident. I told her that it is only normal to cry, be mad, to be sad and to be angry. They are all normal feelings when someone leaves you. I will have these feelings when you leave this world to go to a better place. You have been like family to me and I will always love you and Mickie for all that you have done for me. You will live on in my heart. You are the most caring person that I know and I will never find another like you.

Love you, Ken.

K. H.

June 3ʳᵈ, 2010

Ken, I'm not much for a lot of emotional words, but I just wanted to tell you that you *are* an inspiration to others and to me. I believe you changed my life forever. When I think of people I respect and want to emulate, you are #1 on that list. I do read your updates, even though I don't respond often. I just want you to know that I do care and I'm proud of you for fighting the good fight, for setting the bar and being open and honest during the process. It takes a real man to do what you do.

Sincerely,
A. D.

June 3ʳᵈ, 2010

Do you have any idea how hard it is to see the keyboard when there are tears in my eyes? I marvel at your strength and courage, your gifts of sharing and caring, of teaching and showing us how to live and how to love.

These last four years I have learned so much, about myself, my Godly gifts, from observing you and listening to your words of wisdom and caring. I believe I am a better person and a stronger person. There have been few men who have touched me as you have. God knew, I'm sure, what He had planned when our paths first crossed and thankfully, I was paying attention. I love you, Ken. God's blessings be with you.

R. T.

June 3ʳᵈ, 2010

Your strength amazes me. You are a true teacher in more ways than you know. Lots of hugs from us to you!

J. B.

June 3ʳᵈ, 2010

Thinking of you, Sir. Just a fond memory I have of you from my days back at Finger Lakes: I was practicing IVs (intravenous) at our CC (critical care) class in Hopewell, and you were my "pin cushion". I was having trouble getting it and you grabbed the needle and did it yourself! This is when I got over my fear of needles.

You truly have helped so many. Thank you so much! May God bless!

A. D.

June 3ʳᵈ, 2010

Mr. Kelly, thank you! Because there just isn't enough or the right words to say to you. Thank you!

S. S.

June 4ᵗʰ, 2010

I can only say you are my friend and I love you too.

D. O.

June 4ᵗʰ, 2010

I love you, Kenny.

J. F. F.

June 4ᵗʰ, 2010

Thank you, Ken-Ken.

Your friend,
C. T.

June 5ᵗʰ, 2010

Ken, that poem sure brings tears to the eyes, but how very true it is! Thanks for sharing.

Love,
M. J. H.

June 11ᵗʰ, 2010

Ken, glad to hear you are feeling better. Have a great time on your cruise.

W. G.

June 11ᵗʰ, 2010

Uncle Ken, we continue to pray for you and are always prepared to be there for you in whatever capacity you need us. You are an awesome man, uncle, paramedic, teacher, friend and so many things to so many people. Thank you for being who you are and continuing to be, even when it seems too hard. I love you and I can't wait for our cruise!

Love ya,
A. R.

June 11th, 2010

Ken, I totally agree with my daughter, A., ditto, ditto. We are praying, and eight days left before we sail and party.

T. K.

June 12th, 2010

Enjoy yourself on that cruise and enjoy every minute of the summer. You are one very strong person and you are always in our thoughts and prayers. Have a great time with Mickie and be adventurous.

M. B.

June 12th, 2010

Eight days! I have ordered alcohol for fifty, even though it will just be a few of us. The beast won't know what hit him.

D. O.

June 12th, 2010

Ken, have a great cruise, enjoy every minute, eat everything that looks good to you and Mickie. Drink all your tummy will hold, soak up a ton of sun and make everyone wish they had a tan like yours.

Love to you both,
M. H.

June 12th, 2010

Mr. Kelly, you are a strong man. Keep up your strength and know I pray for your health every day. God bless.

L. L.

June 13th, 2010

Hey Kenny, hang in there, Kiddo. I'm sorry we missed you at B.'s graduation party, but we all know how much you are going through. I was so busy the whole time in Rochester. Sorry I didn't get to see you while I was there. The time flew by too fast. I'm sending lots of love and prayers for your good health and healing.

I hope you have an awesome time on your cruise. I hope the sun, the sea and the ocean smells warm the cockles of your heart and heal your soul. God bless you, cuz.

I love you,
K. L. H.

June 13th, 2010

I forgot to tell you why I was sooo busy. I became the choc-olate-chip-cookie queen while I was there in Rochester. I baked a zillion of them, and because you didn't happen to make it to the graduation party, everyone else had to eat the cookies. I must have made at least eight hundred of them. We all packed on a little weight and clogged arteries from all the butter and sugar. But butter and sugar are good for you, right? They go along with crazy socks too! We ate yours for you just so you two could go off on your cruise and eat all the goodies on the cruise. Enjoy! Lots of hugs and love.

Your Cuz, K. L. H.

June 14ᵗʰ, 2010

Have a great time on your cruise. Rest and relaxation, along with a plethora of frosty cold ones, I believe, are in order.

D. S.

June 14ᵗʰ, 2010

Enjoy your cruise. I hope you have a great time.

L. C.

June 15ᵗʰ, 2010

Hi Kenny, so glad you are feeling better. This weather has been glorious. I hope your cruise is just a blast and you have more fun than you ever have had.

Love you,
J. F. F.

June 16ᵗʰ, 2010

Ken, enjoy and relax on your great vacation. Remember the angel in your pocket!

T. C.

June 29ᵗʰ, 2010

Laughter is, they say, the best medicine.

R. T.

June 29ᵗʰ, 2010

I hope you had a cold beer or two.

D. S.

June 29ᵗʰ, 2010

Thanks for adding joy to my day and thanks for the reminder.

P. F.

June 30ᵗʰ, 2010

Ken, whether you know it or not, I just want to let you know I am truly amazed. How a person who has so much darkness in his life right now, that when I see you, I only see a bright light. You give off a true light of hope and you are living life the same way. We will continue to pray and walk with you. During this trip, you sent out your light onto every one of us and we are so blessed to be part of your life.

Thank you for showing your light to us all and thank you for a great vacation.

T. K.

June 30ᵗʰ, 2010

I can hear your laughter, Kenny. It makes me smile. Glad you had a great time. I thought of you often. Love you.

J. F. F.

June 30ᵗʰ, 2010

Ken, glad to see that you had a great time. A little warm for me now. I like the January and February time frame. It is wonderful that you were able to share this with your loved ones. I am sure they will take more from this trip than just the trip.

I hope things keep going well for you and Mickie. If there is anything that you need, don't hesitate to call or email me.

P. H.

June 30th, 2010

The sharing of meal times, the sharing of drinking times (well that was any time), the just sitting and talking times, seeing you smile, seeing you laugh, seeing you cry—we shared a wonderful week. I thank you for sharing the week with me and L. Let's go again next week! Love you.

D. O.

July 6th, 2010

I took a cruise way back when, I think it was 1991! It was fantastic, and I promised myself to do it again sometime. I'm so glad you got to go with such great friends, and I enjoyed reading about it. It was better than going again myself! I'm so proud for you! Hang in there, Kid!

J. K.

July 8th, 2010

Uncle Ken, I appreciate your honesty and courage to share all these details with us, those that deeply love you. I had so much fun with you on the cruise. Those are memories I will always cherish. I am always here to help you through this, whatever you need. I will continue to pray for you, cry with you, laugh with you, celebrate with you and fight with you.

Love always,
A. R.

July 8th, 2010

Hey, Boss. It fills me with joy to know how exciting, relaxing and rewarding your vacation was. It also provides me with what I will call a little solidarity to know that the beast is under control (not progressing). This is a reflection of your resolve and your courage in this fight. I share with your hopes in many more years. I look forward to seeing you at our celebration in August. God bless, Sir.

J. H.

July 8th, 2010

Dear Ken, you are truly an amazing human being and an inspiration to all who know you! I am in awe of your courage and determination to fight this wretched "beast". God bless you. My love to you and Mickie.

S. W.

July 8th, 2010

There aren't enough words, thoughts, love and prayers for you and your family.

R. T.

July 8ᵗʰ, 2010

Ken, I hope you don't mind the challenge I throw out there to all who are in the medical profession, especially EMS.

When we are dealing with patients that have all their hair and "look good" and are complaining of a fifteen on ten on the pain scale…let's remember Ken. While we are saying how good he looks, underneath it all he isn't feeling that way. He is in pain. We are quick to judge the "pill seekers" that we give care to every day. They may be in real pain. Then there are those that wear diapers, are depressed and downtrodden. Can we be slow to judge and, with care and concern, render care with an understanding heart? It is human nature to judge. We have all fallen prey to that. But it is easier to pull from that curse when we keep our loved ones in mind.

Ken, you will be an inspiration for eons to come! We all consider you a loved one. I thank God for having met you!

D. T.

July 8ᵗʰ, 2010

Uncle Ken, thank you for sharing. I'm glad you were able to join T. and me for dinner. We enjoyed your company. Always know we will be there for you, supporting you and loving you, no matter what.

All our love,
A., R., A. and T. B.

July 8ᵗʰ, 2010

Ken, hang in there and keep fighting. It's a fight worth fighting. Remember all the men and women who have helped shape and educate in this world, myself included. That alone is worth its weight in gold.

W. G.

July 8ᵗʰ, 2010

Ken, thank you for your willingness to let "us" see what you are enduring. You truly are an inspiration. I think of you and pray for you and Mickie often.

J. D.

July 8ᵗʰ, 2010

Ken, I continue to pray for you, Mickie and the docs every night. You are a strong person with an even stronger spirit. It's been some time since my days at FLA, but you are the kindest, most caring and compassionate boss I've ever had. Your strength spread to most of us when we needed it most. You can keep going, Ken. You keep going, and we'll keep praying for you!

"Where the art of medicine is loved, there is also a love of humanity" (Hippocrates).

K. N. B.

July 9ᵗʰ, 2010

Ken, you are a strong person, and I know that you will continue fighting this beast off. Just remember that even though you can't ride in the ambulance, your work is still out there with all the people you have trained to do your work. Each and every one of us has a part of you in us. If it wasn't for you, we would not be able to care for the people who need help. You have taught me a lot, and I will never forget it. So your work continues on in us. Be proud of what you have done up to this point and continue to share your knowledge with us because we never stop learning.

My prayers and love are with you always. You were my dearest friend before you were my teacher. Stay strong, Ken.

K. H.

July 9th, 2010

Ken, my hat is off to you as you travel your bumpy road. I went through almost the same thing that you are going through but not to the degree you are. My worst was the chemo and radiation together and the diarrhea. I wore diapers also, but that saved a lot of embarrassment. My thoughts and prayers are with you and Mickie every day. Do not overdo as it will come back to kick hard. Do cut down and rest as your body tells you. This is just some sisterly advice from someone who had been there.

Love you both,
Just J. L.

July 9th, 2010

Ken, you certainly have a way with words. Having been a student in many of your classes, I knew you could talk well, but I am super impressed with your ability to communicate with the written word. You are in my prayers every day. On Sundays, at the 7:00 a.m. mass at St. Michaels in Penn Yan, the entire church prays for you.

God bless and keep up the good spirit.

Love,
M. H.

July 10th, 2010

Those were mood swings? I thought you were just upset with me again! I will always be there for you. If you need to lean on me sometimes, or if you need help on the steps, that's okay because that's what family and friends are for.

D. O.

July 12ᵗʰ, 2010

In honor of Ken Kelly.

B. C.

July 12ᵗʰ, 2010

Hi, Kenny, you have been in my thoughts every day. Your courage is stunning. Your strength and humility are inspiring. I just want you to know that I love you and am so sorry that you are going through so much pain. I wish I could have helped you with that and take it away. I pray for you and send you all the love I can reach inside of me.

J. F. F.

July 19ᵗʰ, 2010

Ken, I am praying for you today. Know that you are loved and appreciated. May God, give you rest and peace in the midst of this battle.

J. D.

July 19ᵗʰ, 2010

I am thinking of you and sending positive thoughts your way.

J. W.

July 19ᵗʰ, 2010

Stay strong, Ken! We are here for you, just a phone call or email away. If you need anything, just let us know. We love you and are praying for you. You never know how strong you really are. You, my friend, are very strong. You just can't see it right now through all the pain. You are loved by many people, more than you know.

D. Y.

July 19th, 2010

Ken, we are praying for God's grace and mercy for you. May He give you the strength you need. May He be gracious to you and your family.

Regards,
P. F. and Family

July 19th, 2010

Ken, this prayer has always helped me as I struggle and question what happens to the human body. The part I find most inspiring is the power of your hope. God knows that we all reach for Him. Remember to continue to reach and to pray and to *never* give in or to give up.

"May the One who blessed our mothers, may the One who blessed our fathers, hear our prayer and bless us as well. Bless us with the power of Your healing and bless us with the power of Your hope. May our hearts be filled with understanding and strengthened by the power of Your love."

L. R. T.

July 19th, 2010

Ken, I cannot possibly understand the pain that you are in nor will I try. All I can do is, as you wish, pray, which I will, because I am a believer in God's faith and the reward of His heavenly kingdom that awaits all of us!

No one on this earth will ever know the amount or the extent of the pain and suffering that Jesus Christ endured in His last hours before being put to death on the cross. I would dare to say that the amount of pain that you are suffering is similar. I am so sorry that you have to endure such a thing! As I think about it though, it occurred to me that you are doing the same two things that Jesus did to fight the pain. First, it is said that He focused on His Father's promise and concentrated on prayer, thereby *never* losing faith. You are doing that! Second, He continued to teach. You are doing so as well. Every time people read your entries, we learn from you! You inspire all of us!

For the people (like me) who never understood the pain experienced by those who battle this terrible beast, I hope that I (and others) am more compassionate in our care for them in the future. You have made me understand the importance of doing so.

Personally speaking, for the years that I have been blessed to know you (almost twenty now), you taught me things I have not forgotten and have been a true friend and mentor! Having first met you as my ILS (intermediate life support) instructor in 1991, you taught me how to be a professional and confident EMT. This continued through my years as an ALS (advanced life support) provider. You taught me patience while I worked at Finger Lakes Ambulance and told me to "hang in there" when I got frustrated with my career. You convinced the bosses to let me be the first nonsupervisor to operate M-1 in the west end of the county many years ago before OCALS (Ontario County Advanced Life Support) was staffed 24-7. I felt so proud to serve in that capacity and thank you for your faith in me. You taught me how to be an excellent EMS (emergency medical services) instructor and the plaque that I have on the wall of my house is largely due to you and your guidance.

Now, for the past year or so, you continue to teach me (and others) with your words. Your faith is strong! Your courage is astonishing! Jesus taught His disciples how to live a good life and how to care for (love) others as we care for (and love) ourselves. Your life lessons to me and your many other students have been much the same.

Stay strong, my friend! Your friends and family will not abandon you nor will the Lord above! Thank you, Teacher, for all that you have done for me. Your words, your examples and your strength have inspired me forever! I have more to learn! Continue to guide and teach me and thank you for just being you! Amen, I say to you! May the Lord bless and keep you!

I pray for a decrease in your pain and rest for you!

S. D.

July 19th, 2010

I have the faith! I believe! I am with you!

R. T.

July 19th, 2010

We are praying for you and with you. We are here for you and standing beside you. We are ready to do anything you require or need to fight this beast. You have all of our faith, strength and love to use as you need. We believe in God, and we believe in you. All our love and prayers for both you and Mickie.

A. and R. B.

July 19th, 2010

Ken, I wish you comfort during this horrible time. Your words of wisdom have continued to put all of us at ease through everything. I'm not very religious anymore but more spiritual. I respect your connection with your faith and I will pray for you and Mickie that God will bring you both a bit of comfort and relief.

Peace and love,
F. and B. J.O.

July 19ᵗʰ, 2010

Ken, my thoughts and prayers are with you and your family. Prayers for healing for you and the dissolution of your pain. Amen!

D. T.

July 20ᵗʰ, 2010

Ken, words cannot express how we feel for you and how our hearts ache to see and hear of the pain you are in. As many have told you, we are here for you. We are all praying that Jesus will lift this pain from you. You have been so strong and given many of us the strength to do the things we do because you have set such a great example to follow. We are so glad you do continue to write and let us know how you are doing. Just try to remember that Jesus is your strength, your shield and your healer. Even in the darkest places, He is there for you and Mickie. The beast has been defeated. We just have to see what Jesus wants from you. I wish I could tell you, but I know He is there for you.

Call anytime, and we will come, and we will give a hug. We will hold you up, and we will carry you if need be.

Love,
T. and S. K.

July 20ᵗʰ, 2010

Uncle Ken, you are not alone through this. We are praying for your pain to disappear and that God will comfort you physically and emotionally. He will be your strength when you need it. We love you!

A. R.

July 20th, 2010

Dearest Ken, words cannot convey how saddened I am for your pain. You are the bravest person I have ever known. Throughout all of this, you have remained true to our Father. He is with you always, Ken. My prayer for you every day is that you continue to find the strength you need to fight this satanic beast. You are truly an inspiration to all who know you. God bless you and Mickie.

Love,
S. and J. W.

July 20th, 2010

"Cast all your anxiety on Him because He cares for you" (1 Peter 5:7).

J. B.

July 20th, 2010

I am so sorry for your pain, Kenny. I think of you every day and send my love and caring. I love you.

J. F. F.

July 20th, 2010

Kenny, I am so sorry you are in so much pain. There is no need to apologize for your thoughts at this time. I wish there was a way to relieve you. Has anyone talked about a walking epidural? I wish I had an answer for you. I'm hoping you will get over this bump in the road and be back to your electrical antics, your bike and project completion soon. I love you.

L. B.

July 20ᵗʰ, 2010

I hope today finds you feeling a little relief. I pray for you often.

All our love,
L. C.

July 21ˢᵗ, 2010

Thinking of you. Your strength amazes me and also makes me realize that there is a higher power that drives each and every one of us. Ken, keep the strength going.

E. A.

July 21ˢᵗ, 2010

"Come unto Me, all you who are weary and burdened, and I will give you rest." Awesome, Ken, just awesome. Warm hugs and lots of love.

R. T.

July 21ˢᵗ, 2010

Faulkner is one of my favorite writers. I've been fond of him since middle school. I am glad you are ahead of the confines of the beast once again. You have a lot of strength left in you, Sir! I am glad to be a part of this journey with you.

Love and prayers,
J. H.

July 21st, 2010

Welcome back to life, Ken! I agree with you, Faulkner was right. But I disagree with your question of selfishness and the need to say it aloud. It is natural to want the pain to end. It is natural to want to help someone you know that is in pain find relief. It's natural to question yourself and wonder how you can survive it another minute. We are human, which means we have thoughts and questions. It's how we are meant to be. You know, as a medical professional, that pain alters brain function. It's a physical reaction to chemical changes; therefore, you don't have complete control under any kind of stress. My wish for you yesterday was that you would feel better. Today, my wish for you is that you forgive yourself for your perceived faults and sins. Your God loves you. Your family and friends love you. Now if you love yourself completely, including your "flaws", you will be at peace. So that is my wish for you today and always. Peace. I love you.

L. B.

July 21st, 2010

Ken, glad to hear that you are feeling better and are through what sounded to be incredibly horrible, euphemistically speaking. I just returned from a fishing trip to the wilderness of Northern Ontario, Canada. This is where one gets to reflect on how truly great life is and what a magnificent world it is that we live in.

Hang in there, my friend. My thoughts and prayers are with you.

D. S.

July 21st, 2010

Uncle Ken, Amen! Glad to hear you made it through this tunnel and back into the sun. Your last message made me think of one of my favorite songs sung by Bill Withers, "Lean on Me". Have a listen. I know you have heard it before. Music always inspires me. In fact, the other day, "Candy Man" by Sammy Davis Jr. was playing on the radio on my way to work. It put a smile on my face all day just thinking of it. It's such a happy song! In fact, I just Googled it and it made me smile all over again!

I can't possibly understand the full extent of what you are experiencing, but by you sharing the unabridged version of your experience, I find I have a better understanding of what you are going through. This gives me a higher "patience" tolerance for the "patients" I am dealing with. Thank you for sharing and at the same time teaching. Always know we are here for you at all times, no matter what the situation.

All our love,
A. and R. B.

July 21st, 2010

Dear Ken, I know we haven't been very close all these years, but I have been reading all of your posts over these months. I have mostly been at a loss for words for what you have been going through and felt I couldn't contribute much anyway. But your post on Monday drew me into prayer for you as never before. I have seen you draw closer to God and I'm sure cry out to Him through all of this. I just wanted to tell you that I will continue to press into prayer for you as you continue your battle against the beast.

Sincerely,
J. M.

July 21st, 2010

Ken, I have read your journal since you started it and I must say that I admire the strength and endurance that you have shown. It has been said many times in your guestbook and even I have stated the obvious: you have touched so many lives and have done so much good that it pains me to watch you go through this battle.

You have taught me Paramedicine, which was the easy part less all the labs and the countless hours of clinical time. Even now, as I read your post, you teach me how important life and friends are.

As you know, K. lost her mom to the beast, and as our lives have changed by caretaking for her dad, you are even teaching him. Teaching about how life is precious, and no matter what you face, God will make it easier for those who believe in Him.

My friend, I recall all of the times we have worked together. As your birthday approaches, K. and I keep you in our prayers, hoping for peace and comfort for you and your wonderful family.

I wish you peace and joy with every day that we are honored with your presence. As I, and many others have stated before, if you need anything my friend, just ask and I will be happy to help. Even if that is just going to lunch or riding the bike with you. You are a teacher, and even in this great battle, you continue to teach us all to seize the day and live each and every day as if it was our last.

Your student, P. H.

July 22nd, 2010

Ken, so happy to hear that the many prayers for you have been answered! Prayer is much stronger than people realize. Thank you, Teacher, for your continued words of wisdom!

St. Leo once said, *"Prayer has the greatest efficacy to obtain favors from God when it is supported by works of Mercy"*. To all those who sign this guestbook, visit you, hold you, or share a passing smile, these are all testaments of your friends and family's mercy and love for you. Peace to you, my friend!

S. D.

July 22ⁿᵈ, 2010

Ken, you are anything but selfish and I am quite sure that God is saying the same thing. You are an inspiration to myself and to a lot of others as well. Keep fighting, as we are all praying for you.

M. B.

July 22ⁿᵈ, 2010

Uncle Ken, it is wonderful to hear that you are feeling better! I do believe in the power of prayer and of love, both of which you are surrounded by. Little H. has found a new favorite song, which she'd love to sing for you at any time. I am sure you have heard it.

"This is the day, this is the day that the Lord has made. I will rejoice, I will rejoice and be glad in it".

We will continue to celebrate with you, and when you need, we will be here still!

Love,
A. R.

July 23ʳᵈ, 2010

Ken-Ken, you quote Faulkner. I'll quote another famous intellectual: *"Was it over when the Germans bombed Pearl Harbor? Hell no, and it ain't over now"*. (John Belushi as Bluto, *Animal House*)

I hope today is a good one.

C. T.

July 24ᵗʰ, 2010

Kenny, *"The phoenix in all of us arises from the ashes"*! *God bless you.*

What an inspiration and a reminder to all of us you are. Continue to go out, my beloved cousin, to live and love life fully each and every day. This is not a dress rehearsal, so give and take everything you can into each and every moment of each and every day. Forget the mundane and step back and out and aside from it if you can. One step back and one step to the side. You are a constant reminder to me, as is my sister who is also experiencing her challenges in this life lately. Thanks to you both for that little reminder whispering in my ears.

Thank you so much for sharing your journey with us. Helping each and every one of us who love and care about you, gain insight into our own journey into Our Father's House.

Let us all breathe in deeply, breathe out, again, again and again. Relax our bodies, hearts, minds and soul. Stop the chatter and conversations in our heads. Breathe in and out again. Take it slowly, steady, surrounded by awesomeness, trust and love. Walk into that place that is whatever our hearts greatest desire is. Stop and smell the fragrances of the earth and inhale the blessings of this life. Smile as you enjoy and feel safe knowing you are surrounded by complete and total love. Take all the beauty and wonder into our soul. *Smile* as you breathe back in deeply and take in the peace, beauty, freshness and love of those that love you and bring joy and smiles into your life.

Thank you for being part of my life, *all of you*! Please forgive me for getting on my "soapbox". However, I truly believe it is so important for each and every one of us to savor the moments. They can be snatched away so quickly, as especially all of you in the emergency services know. When my heart is touched so much, I feel I must share the love.

May God bless us all.

Love,
K. L. H.

July 26th, 2010

As much as I understand how you felt at your last writing, I knew you would change and go back to the Ken we all know and love. Giving up is not an option you would reach. So happy you are feeling a little better. I can see the pain you are enduring through the days at work. I wish there was something I could do to help ease that pain. Just remember that I will always be there to assist you in any way I can. May God bless!

D. O.

July 27th, 2010

Ken, I hope that the worst is over for you. My thoughts and prayers are with you and Mickie every day. I am sure this is taking a toll on her as she sees you suffering and can't relieve the pain for you. You certainly don't deserve this in my book. God says that he will not give you more suffering than you can bear, and you have sure proved it. Many blessings to you both.

Always,
J. L.

July 27th, 2010

You have been in my mind constantly Kenny, and Mickie too. I talked with L. last week and filled her in so you have even more prayers and love coming to you from your family. I have been trying to decide what to say to you to acknowledge your birthday. What I want to say is that, the world is a better place because you have been present and walking the roads of this experience we call life. I send you love and happiness that you are feeling better. Also, great joy that you "are" feeling better. Birthday blessings to you dear cousin. I love you.

J. F. F.

August 7th*, 2010*

Prayers everyday for you, Sir. You are a true example of strength and courage. You may have followed the example of others but know, others will follow yours. God bless you!

K. G.

August 9th*, 2010*

Ken, thank you for your thoughts, words and encouragements that have taught the rest of us love this last year!

Love,
B. M.

August 12th*, 2010*

Hi Kenny, I'm thankful to read that you are doing better. I can't even begin to imagine what you are going through. It is a great picture of you and Mickie on your last entry. I just wanted to check in and tell you I love you and that you are always in my thoughts and prayers.

K. L. H.

August 15th*, 2010*

None of us has a guarantee about tomorrow. We are blessed to have this day. I am blessed to have you. Love you!

J. F. F.

August 19ᵗʰ, 2010

Dear Uncle Ken, I am thinking of you and praying for you. I wanted to let you know you are loved and you are not alone. Have a good day! XOXO.

A. R.

August 20ᵗʰ, 2010

It is great to read your good news; and it is even better to read of your feelings, your happiness and of your upcoming plans. I sit here looking eight days into the future at my wedding and I am hoping to see you there. Your love of love itself, life and happiness will make it that much more of a joyful day. God bless you, Sir!

With love,
J. H.

August 20ᵗʰ, 2010

Hi Ken, if you will be in Wisconsin during your Midwest trip, let me know. We'd love to see both of you.

P. F.

August 20ᵗʰ, 2010

Ken, I read your updates and am inspired. I'm glad you share as much with us as you do. Not much on sappiness, but I want you to know I'm thinking of you. You are much more than a teacher, mentor, father, friend, uncle, boss, etc. You are a walking real-life hero to so many.

I hope there are more days of happiness and peace than pain. I hope the days of pain are easily controlled. May God continue to bless you and your family and we pray for full healing.

A. D. and family

August 20th, 2010

Hang in there, Kenny. You are surrounded with love and support from us all. You also are an amazing inspiration to us. God bless you and please take it easy!

Lots of love always,
Your Cuz, K. L. H.

August 21st, 2010

Hey Ken, I pray that your pain subsides. We hope you have a great time with Mickie in November on the train trip. I've heard nothing but great things about it. You are one of the strongest men I know and I'm grateful I have you in my life.

Love,
F. and B. J. O.

August 23rd, 2010

No wonder you had so much pain. Glad to hear that you have a rebound time and can look forward to that as a rope to pull you out of the well when it gets overwhelming. The train trip sounds exciting! You always have so much reenergizing when you have something special to look forward to. Glad to hear today is a good day! Love you.

J. F. F.

August 25th, 2010

Mr. Kelly, you are in my prayers, and I am so thrilled with your joys and accomplishments. I hope you have a great few weeks.

L. K.

August 30th, 2010

That's all any of us have, dear cousin. I hear the grief in your process and I am sorry for the losses that you are pondering. The poignancy of cherishing the present and celebrating the beauty of each day. Appreciating the love of our life while missing and coming to terms with the loss of our youth is such a rich process. I never appreciated it so deeply when I had endless vigor. I realize that this bittersweet drink of life leads to wisdom. We may not be with wisest, but boy, we take life head on and do our best to grasp the richness. God bless you.

J. F. F.

August 30th, 2010

Ken, you are such an inspiration. I thank God for your good days and ask Him to keep you strong on the bad days. Sending you love and prayers.

S. W.

August 30th, 2010

Resting is forced time to observe the world around you! These are observations you would not have had if you too were bustling by. You are rich in wisdom. Thank you for sharing with us.

J. W.

August 31ˢᵗ, 2010

Ken, you are a great friend and I feel like you are family to me. I will cherish all the memories that we shared. Be strong and God will be with you every step of the way. You and your family are in my prayers. Love you, Ken.

K. H.

August 31ˢᵗ, 2010

Ken, first, we are so happy you and Mickie went to the fair. We know how much you looked forward to going; and even though you may have had to stop and rest, that is okay because you took the steps, one at a time, and still went for it. You are such a light to us all, to see you still do all the things you love to do, maybe slower, but you still are trying to enjoy life. We are so very proud of you. I saw you yesterday and you looked great mowing the lawn. You just keep your eyes on today and let Jesus worry about tomorrow. Great song to start your day. Praying for you always and for Mickie also. God bless you.

T. K.

August 31ˢᵗ, 2010

Our prayers and our love,

S. and R. T.

September 3ʳᵈ, 2010

Hi, Ken, here's to spending together tomorrow with J.'s family. We will have a great time. D. said, "Tell Grammy I don't have to eat clams, okay?" I guess that's just more for you and me. XOXO.

L. M. Y.

September 5th, 2010

Ken, what you think and how you feel are part of the miracle called Ken Kelly. As I have said previously, your words have brought me tears, smiles, encouragement and an outpouring of love for you, your struggle and you as a fellow human being.

Your melancholy is a process. It is yours to express in whatever way you choose. Those of us that love you and respect you will find no fault. We continue to love, support and pray with you as you continue to teach us how to live. No apologies needed!

R. T.

September 5th, 2010

Keep up the good fight, Sir. Not all of us may be able to fully understand what you are going through, but we are here to support you and help in any way we can. The more morose and melancholier you feel, the more we are here to help and listen, also to hold a hand or offer a shoulder in your time of need. We may not have the answers you are seeking, but there is plenty of love and support here to help you along your quest.

M. G.

September 6th, 2010

Hey Ken and Mickie, wishing you guys had a great Labor Day, maybe a picnic or barbeque with good friends and family. It's a great night for sitting outside, and hopefully, you're sucking up the good days before the snow falls. All our love and support.

F. and B. J. O. (and Stu Dog)

September 7ᵗʰ, 2010

Hi Ken, I just wanted to send you my love and support and also to thank you from the bottom of my heart. You fight this fight every single day. You fight it with a million of us standing next to you. But you, of course, are our leader. You are brave. You are selfless. You are a force of nature. You are strong yet humble. Thank you for being the best person I know. Thank you for being J.'s best friend. Thank you for being D.'s "bestest" hero. Having you in our lives makes us rich beyond compare.

Love,
L., J. and D. Y.

September 11ᵗʰ, 2010

Hey Uncle Ken, I hope you're doing well. You've been on my mind a lot lately. I wanted to see how you've been doing and how your summer has been. I wanted to let you know that I love you, those three words you can never say too often.

While reading your posts, I saw that you got discouraged when you realized how much you still wanted to do. All I can say is, "Carpe diem". No matter who you are or how much time you have left, no one can accomplish everything they want to do. All you can do is enjoy everything you have done, are able to do and share it with the people you love. I can't wait to see you while I'm home for Christmas. I hope you have a wonderful September and enjoy what's left of the summer days before the winter arrives.

T. B.

September 13ᵗʰ, 2010

Dearest Ken, God is with you, now and as He has been always. *"Let not your heart be troubled. Trust in God, trust also in Me. In my Father's house are many rooms, if it were not so, I would have told you.*

197

I am going there to prepare a place for you. If I go and prepare a place for you, I will come back and take you to be with me that you also may be where I am. You know the way to the place where I am going" (John 14:1–3).

We are here for you, Ken. Feel free to lean on us, your friends and your family.

P. H.

September 13th, 2010

Ken, thoughts and prayers are being lifted up for you right now. May the Lord God, your Maker, hear and attend to your need in this hour. May the enemy of your soul be kept far from you and your thought process. He comes to seek, steal and destroy, but you belong to your Maker, who promised *never* to leave you. I am praying for physical and mental rest for you tonight, Ken. Don't be afraid to rest in Him.

T. H.

September 13th, 2010

Ken, you have been through so much. This we all know, your friends and family who love you so very much. You are allowed to have dark moments. But know that when the light enters your life, you will see all of us there for you, because we are all here for you, not only in the light but also during those dark moments. You are not alone while you go through this.

We all pray for you and send good thoughts your way. I haven't known you very long, only a few years, but in those years, I have come to care about you and look forward to the barbeques with the Y.'s family. You are family to me, and I cherish that.

Stay strong, Ken. We all love you.

D. Y.

September 13th, 2010

Once again, though under A.'s name, I have come to visit. It is C. D. I get your updates from her, but sometimes I feel the need to connect with you myself and read your words. Though I realize we really don't know each other well, I have truly hung on your every word of wisdom and insights into life and the ways of humans. My gift of empathy usually leaves me in tears when I am done reading. Some are in awe of how amazing you are in your battle. Some are feeling your pain and anguish on the bad days. I think of you more often than you know, Mr. Kelly. I may not be able to do much to help you, but I can give you the gift of knowing your words do make a difference to me. They teach me how to be a better person, a stronger person and a more compassionate person. I wish to thank *you* for taking the time to write and for taking that gift of another day. Each day you choose to fight gives us more to learn about what genuine goodness is all about.

Thank you for being you, Mr. Kelly. I will never be able to address you as Ken. It just seems disrespectful compared to the level of respect I have for you.

C. D. and A. K.

September 13th, 2010

"When I looked in the sand, Lord, I saw only one set of footprints. This was at my darkest time, in my deepest depression. How could you leave me at my hardest times, Lord?

It was then that my Lord looked upon my face and smiled. He said to me, 'Child, when you see one set of footprints, it was then that I carried you.'"

I will pray for you tonight, Ken.

K. N. B.

September 13th, 2010

Ken, my thoughts and prayers are with you! I hope that you find comfort in your friends and family. You have been there for us so many times, it is time for us to be there for you. Keep your faith in God, for He will lead you in your journey. He will not lead you astray. A wise friend once told me, "*I can do all things through Christ who strengthens me*," and I believe we both can!

Always,
A. M.

September 13th, 2010

Ken, our hearts ache for you, we so wish we could do something to help you. We so wish we could take the pain away, and we could heal you. Only our mighty Lord Jesus can do that; and we cry out every day and ask *why, why*, Ken. Lord, please take the pain away. Please heal him. We will continue to ask this until we receive an answer. Just know we are all standing with you, even when you feel so all alone. Don't say you are sorry for what you write; that is what this is for. We all understand and know you have good days and bad days and we want to hear about how you are doing. We all love and care for you and Mickie.

Praying your week will be better than this past week was.

Love,
T. K.

September 13th, 2010

Dear Ken, you are in my thoughts and prayers always.

S. W.

September 13th, 2010

Ken, thinking of you often and so glad to see you at work each day. Your fight is an inspiration.

B. C.

September 13th, 2010

We will be praying for you. You looked great yesterday, and it was fun to see you laugh.

S. P.

September 13th, 2010

Dear Lord Jesus, I pray that you will reach down and touch Ken with Your peace, Your love, Your joy and Your healing power. Give him faith when he feels low and far from You. Lead him into Your presence Lord. Help him to lean on You and not on his own understanding! We praise You, and we praise Your name. In Jesus's name we pray, Amen.

J. M.

September 13th, 2010

We are all with you, hear your fears and brush away your tears. Lean on us. That is what we are here for. We will be your strength when you have none left. We will pick you up when you fall and we will be your shoulder to cry on when you need it. Most importantly, we are your friends and will always be here for you and your family.

Never apologize for voicing your fears for it shows you are human and everyone needs help at times.

Much love always,
J., D. and little M. B.

September 13th, 2010

Please know you are in my thoughts. Dark moments, hours or days are expected. The dark will eventually give way to the light.

J. W.

September 14th, 2010

Ken, my thoughts and prayers are with you, my friend. May you find the strength to make the climb back.

Always,
D. S.

September 14th, 2010

Ken, sorry to hear you are feeling down, but you have the right to. I know you will bounce back and be in a better frame of mind soon. Remember your family and friends are always here for you.

W. G.

September 14th, 2010

Friends are friends through the dark and difficult times as well as in the moments of laughter and with a cold beer for you! We are here for you, to listen, to love, to pray and to comfort you when you need us. Not only today but always. Love you, Ken.

R. T.

September 14th, 2010

Hi Ken! I hope this message finds you with a bit less pain that you had while drafting your last entry. The way you wear your heart on your sleeve helps me understand more and more each day how precious life is and how important it is to embrace the smallest (which turn out to be the largest) things. I listen to you as you take us all on this journey with you, and you end up giving us all strength and a better understanding of just how strong people can be with a little faith, some good friends and a great family.

F. and I were feeling a bit lost recently as we brought his mother up here to live with us. It has taken a lot of adjusting as it's been difficult learning how to be an at-home caregiver for a loved one. We have the challenges of having an eighty-three-year-old "child" so to speak. She has an opinion on everything and "mother superior" knows it! She's is great though. We are learning patience and tolerance that most people gain from child-rearing. In the past two months, we have finally had the experience of having a real family, participating in dinner planning, budgeting and learning about community resources to provide entertainment with folks her own age. Now I understand some of the things you talk about when you speak about family.

If you ever want to come and sit on the river and have a beer with F.'s mother, then just let me know. It's a relaxing setting, and watching the giant fish jump is peaceful.

You are one of the strongest men I know. Thinking of you and Mickie.

B. J. O.

September 14*th*, 2010

Ken, you will always have our prayers with you. We often think about the strong person that you are, but even a strong person has moments of weakness. It is called being human. If you need someone to talk to or even someone just to listen, you know where to find us. We will be here for you. God bless you.

M. B.

September 14*th*, 2010

Hi Ken, it was great to see you out on Saturday. I'm so sorry to hear that the pain has returned and that you are struggling so much. I will be thinking of you and praying for you and Mickie over the coming days.

J. D.

September 14*th*, 2010

Hi Ken. I am sorry you are in so much pain. I hope that knowing so many people love and care for you helps. We are all praying for you. I hope you have had some relief from the pain. God is with you and will not abandon you. We are all beside you with all of our love and support.

L. C.

September 14*th*, 2010

He is with you, and we are with you.

C. T.

September 14th, 2010

Dearest best boss I ever had in the world, you are not alone. I promise to raise you up each day and be consistent in my fight with your beast in prayer and thought. You will have sunny days, and you will sleep the sleep of rest and peace each night, because God will *not* abandon you in your time! He has raised up warriors around the world and this country to be in constant battle for you, and I will be one of many. The Word says that if I can put one thousand to flight, can you imagine what thousands can do? Keep us posted!

D. T.

September 14th, 2010

My dearest Ken, you are not alone, not ever. You are in my thoughts all the time. You are in my heart every beat that is has. I am here for you no matter what. Please know you are loved and we are all here for you. Lean on all of us, and let this beast know it is not any match for the powerful love and friendship we share.

J., L. and D.Y.

September 14th, 2010

Mr. Kelly, my thoughts and prayers are with you always. I am so sorry to hear that you have fallen into the depths of sorrow and depression. I am always here for a shoulder or an ear.

Hugs always,
L. K.

September 14th, 2010

Uncle Ken, I attended a wedding this past weekend, and it was beautiful. Although I was there for the bride and groom, sitting in the church, listening to the ceremony, I was thinking of you. The bride's son gave a reading (he was so cute!) from 1 Corinthians 13:4, *"Love is patient, love is kind. It does not envy, it does not boast, it is not proud. It is not rude, it is not self-seeking, it is not easily angered, it keeps no record of wrongs. Love does not delight in evil but rejoices with the truth. It always protects, always trusts, always hope, always perseveres."* Later in verse 13, *"And now these three remain; faith, hope and love. But the greatest of these is love"*.

You have given so much of that spoken love to so many. I for one have experienced it. Believe in your love and all the love that is coming back to you from all of us here. This love will lead you out of the darkness. Although you can't see it in the dark, feel it. It is there for you.

I am praying for you and think of you every day. Know you are not alone in the dark.

All my love,
A. B.

September 15th, 2010

Hi Uncle Ken, I just wanted you to know I think about you and I'm sorry the journey is a struggle right now. You are blessed to have so many who care very deeply for you, and I wish there were some way that we could help you carry this heavy burden. Know that I love you and I'm with you in spirit, if not presence. I read this poem the other day in a book and I thought of you:

When things go wrong, as they sometimes will, when
the road you're trudging seems all uphill.
When the funds are low and the debts are high, and
you want to smile, but you have to sigh.
When care is pressing you down a bit, rest if you
must, but don't you quit.
Life is queer with its twists and turns, as every one
of us sometimes learns,

*And many a failure turns about, when he might
    have won had he struck it out.*
*Don't give up though the pace seems slow, you may
    succeed with another blow.*
*Often the goal is nearer than it seems to a faint and
    faltering man,*
*Often the struggler has given up, when he might
    have captured the victor's cup*
*And he learned too late when the night slipped
    down, how close he was to the golden crown.*
*Success is failure turned inside out, the silver tint of
    the clouds of doubt,*
*And you never can tell how close you are, it may be
    near when it seems so far.*
*So, stick to the fight when you're hardest hit, it's when
    things seem worst that you must not quit.*

Don't quit, Uncle Ken, we're all rooting for you and are behind
you supporting you and loving you every step of this long journey.

Love always,
A. B.

September 17th, 2010

Dear Ken, I'm sorry you are in such pain, physical and spiritual.
I am concerned that your spiritual beliefs are not comforting you at
this time. I can't say that I understand, but I know you have myri-
ads of thoughts racing through your mind. I'd like to point out that
you are surrounded by people who love you and are waiting for any
chance they can find to return the kindness and love you have shown
them. You have always been a giver, and now it's time to receive.
Even in your accepting love, kind wishes or help, you will still be
giving, because everyone is looking for a way to repay the kindness
you have shown. You have worked so hard all your life. You have
achieved amazing heights, helped thousands and thousands of people

directly and indirectly. So if this fight drains you so much, would it be wrong to focus your energy on yourself, just like you've told so many others to do for themselves? What about riding your bike all day long if you want, not just before seven in the morning and after three in the afternoon? What about a walk in the park on a week day? What about just relaxing? I know you don't want to put anyone out, but I'm certain that no matter what happens, you couldn't convince anyone around you that you are a burden.

I realize there is more to your pain than this which I can't speak to. I recognize that you are much harder on yourself than anyone else would be, including your God, I think. It's okay to have weak moments, it's okay to accept a helping hand and it's okay to say when you've had enough. Just as it's okay to laugh, play, relax and nurture yourself. It seems like it's time for you to take care of yourself the way you have always cared for others and to let others care for you just as you have for them. Remember to love, laugh and live! PS I love you.

L. B.

September 17th, 2010

You are in my thoughts and prayers, Ken. You are a great man who has done great things. Your life is greatly appreciated by every person you have men. Thank you for everything. May God bless you.

K. G.

September 19th, 2010

Take my hand and I will help you climb, or take my hand and we will sit and rest. My thoughts are always with you.

D. O.

September 20th, 2010

Ken, I am praying today you are well and your conference went well. Pray you have a safe trip back home. I just wanted you to know we are praying for you and hope to see you soon.

T. K.

September 25th, 2010

I love you!

C. B.

October 1st, 2010

Dearest Ken, you are the most courageous person I know. You are a blessing to all those who know and love you. Please remember that you are forever in my prayers. God loves you, Ken. He is always with you.

S. W.

October 1st, 2010

Hey Boss, I still marvel at your strength. When most would cower and hide in fear, you press forward. You still are an inspiration. There isn't anything in this world I would not give to make all of this go away for you. As I have said before, and I am sure others have said to you, you are like a second father to me. You have always guided me, believed in me. You have been there to answer questions, offer support and join in celebration. My heart aches for your suffering. My tears fall in sadness for your pain and struggles. My prayers flow like a river asking God to comfort you and be with you wherever your journey may take you.

I pray that both your spiritual and physical strength both continue to prevail. I offer any support to you or your family that I can. I will come and burn leaves with you in your backyard, share some wheat beers with you or just share conversation with you.

You inspire me. If I turn into half the man you are, half the paramedic you are, I will be okay.

J. H.

October 1ˢᵗ, 2010

If I could: If I could give you a miracle, I would. If I could take away the pain, I would. If I could take the chemo and radiation for you, I would. If I could give you any wish you wanted, I would. If I could give you all of my strength, I would.

But all I can do is pray, so praying is what I do. Because there is someone who can do all of those things I could not!

J. B.

October 1ˢᵗ, 2010

Ken, in addition to everything I've said prior to this, *I love you*!

J. H.

October 1ˢᵗ, 2010

I will not quit on you. I love you.

A. B.

October 1st, 2010

Amen, Cousin. Without your work, your family, friends and the gift of caring, there would be no point. I support you completely. You have your priorities straight. I love you.

J. F. F

October 1st, 2010

Ken, I'm sorry to read this latest entry. May the Lord hold you in His loving arms as you face this news. May your faith keep you focused.

C. S.

October 1st, 2010

Ken, God didn't promise days without pain, laughter without sorrow nor sun without rain. But He did promise strength for the day, comfort for the tears and light for the way. Thank you for not quitting! We will not quit on you! Hold that angel in your pocket tight and do not let go!

T. C.

October 2nd, 2010

You are first and foremost my friend and my teacher. I pray for you. I love you, Ken.

R. T.

October 2ⁿᵈ, 2010

Praying for you, Ken.

L. M.

October 4ᵗʰ, 2010

Ken, I am a firm believer that God does not give us more than we can handle. We do not always like what He gives us, but that is not our choice. I will continue to pray for you, and I will not quit. You are one of the strongest people that I know. You always think of others before yourself. All my love and prayers to you, and I know that you will not quit. Stay strong.

M. B.

October 4ᵗʰ, 2010

"Never ever, ever, ever, ever, ever, ever give up. Never give up. Never give up. Never give up" (Winston Churchill, October 29ᵗʰ, 1941, at the Harrow School).

D. S.

October 5ᵗʰ, 2010

Ken, keep writing or have someone do the typing for you. Don't ever worry about getting any of us down. Your strength, devotion and drive are powerful and a huge inspiration. *Thank you!*

J. K.

October 5th, 2010

Dear Kenny, lots and lots of love and prayers are coming your way. You are such a good person and always have been. I truly am sorry you have to suffer so much. You are an incredible teacher in so many ways.

God bless you and much love always,
K. L. H.

October 8th, 2010

Mr. Kelly, don't give up and stay strong. Fear is only possible if you let it plague your mind. Big hugs!

L. K.

October 12th, 2010

Hi Ken, I was thinking about you and hope you are having a good day. I will see you tomorrow at the Training and Ed Meeting.

L. W.

October 13th, 2010

With you always, my friend.

D. O.

October 17th, 2010

God, in all His mercy, has forgiven. Now forgive yourself. Ask and ye shall receive.

R. T.

October 17th, 2010

Dearest Ken, God has most assuredly forgiven you. You have so redeemed yourself with all the good that you have done with your life and for others. You are in my thoughts and prayers.

S. W.

October 17th, 2010

Ken, take some comfort in the fact that you saw the good in me at a time in my life when it was difficult for people to do so. You treated me more than fairly at times, and I likely did not deserve such treatment. I am forever grateful to have known and worked with you.

C. T.

October 17th, 2010

Ken, I cannot help but to be humbled that you allow me the honor and privilege of sharing your difficult journey and innermost thoughts. As much as I hate to admit it, you brought me to tears today and affirmed the pride and faith I have in you as well. We have all done things we regret. I'm sure you already know what I'm telling you next, but if not, I hope it helps. The Bible says we must turn from our evil ways and repent, ask for forgiveness and it will be given. I firmly believe in that because Jesus did die for our sins so that all may be forgiven.

I sincerely will pray for you today and pray for healing. I don't promise that to many because I forget to pray later. I promise you I will pray for peace and healing in you. For your eternal peace and healing of your heart and soul as well as for your physical restoration.

Ever since I met you and was scared to death the first interview for paramedic school, I felt I had found a real hero and mentor. I know you hate hearing that from your students because *you* still consider yourself as one of us. But all that you do is like a beacon on a hill! Thank you again for the tears, for the inspiration, for the example and also for sharing with the rest of us!

A. D.

October 17ᵗʰ, 2010

Thank you for sharing such intimate stories about your life. Although we cannot change the past, we can certainly learn from it. Thank you for encouraging us with your words of wisdom, strength and endurance. God only gives us what He knows we can handle. Keep fighting and know that we are all here for you whenever you need us.

L. R.

October 17ᵗʰ, 2010

Dear Ken, we just want to say again how much we care about you and Mickie. Your faith inspires us. Your words comfort and teach us. I wish you a little bit of peace and a bit of time without the pain.

All our love,
F. and B. J. O.

October 17ᵗʰ, 2010

Uncle Ken, we celebrate the good news and continue to pray for you and the guidance of your doctors!

I am a firm believer that God forgives us if we admit our sin and ask for forgiveness. You are a very good man and have done so much good for others. For myself, personally, you have helped me out more times than I can count on both hands and toes included! How many times since that incident on the playground have you looked into someone's crying eyes and offered them comfort when they were scared or hurt?

You had just recently spoken about embracing moments. We are all guilty of being too busy or too tired at one time or another when we could have embraced that moment. Grandma loved you so much. If you asked her today, she would only remember all the good you have done for her. You made sacrifices to take care of her and the family. She would be so very proud of you and your strength as all of us are.

Thank you for sharing with us. I hope it continues to be a source of comfort to you. You are loved immensely!

Love always,
A. R.

October 18th, 2010

Hey, Ken, I'm pretty sure you will be forgiven for your two mistakes. First of all, kids will be kids. At that age, you do not have executive functioning to make adult decisions. The important thing is, that you realized it was wrong and changed your behavior. As for the Christmas lights, you have to let that one go. First of all, you had a long day and obviously needed to take care of yourself. More importantly, you were there for your mother and taking care of her. She didn't have to walk to the doctor and she didn't have to skip the doctor. Knowing her, I'm sure that even though she was a little disappointed, if it was a very important thing, she would have communicated that to you. Again, you learned from it and in my belief, that is the important issue in forgiveness. Humans make mistakes. It's those who repeat them intentionally that will have a problem when sins are being counted. Let it go and don't waste another moment of your life worrying about one-time mistakes. Make every moment count.

L. B.

October 22ⁿᵈ, 2010

Ken, we all have things we regret, but we all know how much you loved Ma and how you took care of her most of your life. She loved you as well. Don't hold on to the regrets, put them in God's hands and remember all the good. Do not let the regrets rob you of all the good times you had with her.

Love,
T. K.

October 26ᵗʰ, 2010

Ken boy, did your story about your mother and the Christmas lights hit home. I did the identical thing Christmas of 2001. That was one of my mother's few joys life in life (she was eighty-five), and I didn't have the time to take her for a ride around Penn Yan to look at the beautiful Christmas lights. God is making me painfully aware of my misdeed each and every Christmas since. She died February 2002. Now God sent me another little dart with your story.

The rest of your latest news bulletin sounds quite positive. Maybe the prayers from Penn Yan are helping a little.

Love,
M. H.

October 27ᵗʰ, 2010

Mr. Kelly, one of my dearest friend's fathers was just diagnosed with lung cancer. He is starting chemo and radiation this week. It is really scary. He is surprisingly optimistic.

Thank you so much for the constant updates. You are always in my prayers and thoughts.

L. K.

November 2nd, 2010

Hi, Ken, you never cease to amaze me with your thoughts. You continue to amaze me with your courage. You have blessed us all by allowing us to share this "journey" with you. You are sharing the good parts and the not so good parts. May God continue to give you the strength you need to fight the beast. May He continue to hold you in His hands and give you comfort. You are in my thoughts and prayers every day, Ken—and Mickie too.

Love,
S. and J. W.

November 2nd, 200

Dear Kenny, I just wanted to tell you that you are always in my thoughts and prayers. You are such an incredible inspiration in bravery, humanity, love and friendship to all of us who are fortunate enough to be part of this journey with you. We are surrounding you with love and support. Thank you for your thoughts and sharing your feelings and inspirations that come with this journey with the "beast". Your honesty and feelings help us all to become braver in our own journey. With you we all are growing. May God bless you, kiddo, and lots of love to Mickie and the rest of the family too.

K. L. H.

November 3rd, 2010

Ken, not a day goes by that I am not thinking of you and Mickie. What a wonderful couple and friend you have been to me and my family. I am sorry that I didn't realize the love that was given many years ago as accepting me as part of the family. As I get older, I realize that I am alone as far as brothers and sisters go. I could have had it all. Funny how we think of many things as we get older and realize what could have been.

My love and support are with you and Mickie every day!

J. L.

November 5th, 2010

I will call. What I know is that a heart that seeks forgiveness is immediately forgiven. The hardest part is learning to forgive ourselves. I know your mom would laugh and say, "Oh, Honey, don't be silly. Of course, I forgive you". It would pain her more to know you feel such terrible shame over a very human reaction. We aren't perfect, Kenny, just "good enough". We say we know more than God when we hold on to the lack of self-forgiveness, because God's grace is instant and unwavering. Your childhood act was just that, the act of a child. A childish choice. You scared him, you didn't kill him. Let it go.

J. F. F.

November 5th, 2010

Ken, our thoughts and prayers are with you. Stay positive.

W. G.

November 5th, 2010

God bless you Mr. Kelly and a speedy recovery. May God be near you during this time.

L. K.

November 6th, 2010

Thank you for continuing to share your life with us, for reminding us of where our true treasures lie. Our prayers will continue to flow for you and your family.

L. O.

November 6th, 2010

T. and I are praying for you. We are amazed at the way you bounce back each time and look forward to hearing you bounce back from this also.

J. D.

November 7th, 2010

Sending lots of prayers your way.

Love
J., D. and M. B.

November 8th, 2010

Prayers are with you, my friend.

D. S.

November 8th, 2010

Hello my dear friend, it has been a while since I have visited your site. I tend to be better on the phone, texting or, my personal favorite, visiting you. It makes me so happy to know that you have a virtual army of love and support that surrounds you. You are a truly wonderful man. I was perplexed reading your entry regarding Miss

G. and the Christmas lights. Don't think that one moment in time defines your relationship with your mom. I can honestly tell you that, as a mom, she would never have given that moment as much weight as you did. When a child, no matter what age, inadvertently disappoints or unintentionally hurts their mom, the pain only lasts a split second. Moms are coated in a special kind of armor that allows them to be a mom. That armor is made from love. Ken, Miss G. had many, many layers of armor. Don't you think on that Christmas light story again. You are a wonderful son.

We love you,
L., J. and D. Y.

November 12th, 2010

In honor of Ken Kelly. Thank you for being so brave. Thank you for Caring Bridge so we can pass on our love, prayers and support to you.

K. L. H.

November 12th, 2010

Ken, you are always in my thoughts and prayers.

E. Z. (Y.)

November 12th, 2010

Bless you, Kenny. You are awesome.

Love,
K. L. H.

November 12th, 2010

Ken, as I read each of your posts, I know that I am wiser for knowing you. I am enriched in ways that no person can understand for knowing you. I could only hope that, faced with what you are faced with, I could be so brave and so full of life. While your time may be shortened with us, your gift to mankind will live on for many years.

You, my friend, have made one of the greatest gifts possible to this earth. You have educated. You have ensured that, through your work, mankind has been made better. If we all could live to that standard, imagine what life would be like.

Prayers continue to go out to you from K. and I. Hopefully, He will comfort you and provide you with many more peaceful days.

P. H.

November 12th, 2010

Thank you for sharing your life with us.

J. W.

November 13th, 2010

Ken, each time I read a message from you, I look at life in a different way. You have opened so many of your friends and family members eyes to the importance of each day and how not to waste it. I thank you for that. You have planted so many seeds in friends and family and even in just people you talk to in your life so far. You may not see it, but there are orchards of fruit out there getting ready to fall into a new look at life. There are fields of flowers blossoming because of how you have touched people's lives. I truly hope that you see that in some of the people you see each day. I love hearing from your heart.

T. K.

November 14ᵗʰ, 2010

I am not on the computer often, so I get news a lot slower than most. I heard that you had an issue about a week ago. I hope that things are okay. I also hope that the train trip is the best.

Love always,
D. K.

November 14ᵗʰ, 2010

Ken, your words are an inspiration to us all. I will follow your lead and live each day to its fullest, helping those I can along the way. My best to you and Mickie.

L. (D.) B.

November 14ᵗʰ, 2010

You have already delivered so many blossoms! I hope you can feel satisfied that you have planted much. *We* have no control over what happens next, but you have lived more than most humans. By having faced this ultimate set of choices, your every moment is spent consciously. I hope you can let in the gift of knowing you have done your best, *really* done your best, and it mattered. I love you.

J. F. F.

November 18ᵗʰ, 2010

That is a great lesson for us all to remember. My love and prayers to you, Ken.

K. G.

November 22ⁿᵈ, 2010

My prayers are with you Ken. Your writing is beautiful and very touching. There are many things that can be learned from your entries.

> Your friend,
> A. E.

December 16ᵗʰ, 2010

Ken, you have been on my heart these couple of days. I have wanted to say that we are praying for you. I want to thank you for opening my eyes to so much this past year.

> Love,
> T. K.

December 19ᵗʰ, 2010

Ken, you are a very strong person, and I know that you will keep fighting the beast, forever if need be. May God bless you and look after you.

> M. B.

December 20ᵗʰ, 2010

Mr. Kelly, I truly am amazed at your courage and strength. I am glad the doctors gave you a rest from chemo during Christmas so you can enjoy the time with your family. God bless you.

> L. K.

December 21st, 2010

Well said my friend.

D. O.

December 21st, 2010

Ken, we all have fight in us when needed. Strength does come in many ways. Give that angel in your pocket a little tighter squeeze and go forward fighting and living!

Hugs to you!

T. C.

December 22nd, 2010

Ken, you are a pillar of strength for all of us. When things get tough, I look at how you are fighting and what you are going through, and I hold my head high and push on. My wish for everyone for the holiday season is that everyone gets to spend time with their loved ones and cherish every single moment. Merry Christmas to you and Mickie.

All our love always,
J., D. and M. B.

December 30th, 2010

Ken, on December 9th, I was informed I have lung cancer. On January 4th, I will find out if it is operable. On December 19th, I found my sister dead in her TV chair and on December 23rd, I buried her. It's been a great holiday season.

Keep up your words of encouragement in your journal. I do love them.

M. H.

January 5th, 2011

We are praying for you!

S. P.

January 5th, 2011

Thank you for sharing with us. Your courage inspires me. I love you.

J. F. F.

January 5th, 2011

Once again, thank you for your honesty and sharing. I wish I could give back to you some of the strength and inspiration I get when I read your thoughts. We continue to pray for you.

P. F.

January 5th, 2011

Uncle Ken, my heart is saddened to hear that your day has been tough. My wish is for the rest of your day to be wonderful and you can continue to stay ahead of the beast. All I can offer is prayers, hugs, love and friendship. I give it all to you wholeheartedly.

With much love,
A. R.

January 5ᵗʰ, 2011

Dear Ken, I pray your faith in the Almighty continues to fuel your resolve to fight the wretched beast. You are such an inspiration to all who have read your journal or to those lucky enough to know you personally!

God bless you, Ken. Keep up the fight.

Love,
S. and J. W.

January 5ᵗʰ, 2011

Ken, praying for you and for relief from the pain. You are a very strong person and battle well, but don't forget, "the battle belongs to the Lord" and He's got you covered. Rest in Him and be strengthened, dear friend. I continue to storm the Throne for Grace and Mercy for you.

T. H.

January 7ᵗʰ, 2011

Still here praying for you. Stay strong!

Love,
J., D. and M. B.

January 19ᵗʰ, 2011

Ken, I have missed your words of wisdom! Some days when I am feeling low, I will look back here and read your words. Not to see your battle, but to read your words of encouragement. You encourage me to look at life from a different view as I struggle within myself sometimes. I cherish your words. Today is one of my low days, and it must be you sensed it! Thank you. I will be thinking of you today as you go another round with this beast. Sending hugs!

L. C.

January 19ᵗʰ, 2011

Good luck with this round of chemo, Kenny. I love you.

L. B.

January 19ᵗʰ, 2011

My dear Ken, I just finished reading your entry. What a terrific time D. had with his Uncle Ken too. His love for you is pure and unwavering. You are his hero and best buddy. He is a very special boy and I am so proud of the relationship you and he have. From the day he came into our lives, he has known his Uncle Ken. He has learned so many things from you and how you live your life. Among them are to be honest, forthright, nonjudgmental, generous, fearless, loving and to be of service to others. He is a remarkable boy. Know that it is in part because of you. That being said, he has also gotten away with bloody murder with you and had far too many cookies! Oh well, nobody is perfect!

We love you,
J., L. and D. Y.

January 20ᵗʰ, 2011

Ken, reading your words has brought me to open my eyes to what I have in front of me, a loving husband, children and grand-children. I feel that I live on to cherish every moment with them. You have taught me many things, and to this day, I am still learning from you. Don't stop teaching. We have a lot to learn from you.

Love,
K. H.

January 25th, 2011

You are an amazing person and can conquer when others fail. Keep fighting. You have so many people by your side.

Love,
J., D. and M. B.

January 27th, 2011

In honor of Ken Kelly, a friend and a leader I aspire to emulate.

M. H.

February 11th, 2011

Oh KWK, we, as in your wife, your kitty, Poko, J, myself and D. are relaxing in your home. We have had a beautiful evening together as a family. We had pizza and wings and a great movie. What I want to point your attention to is that "my family" is so sad about Sampson, but you have made it a beautiful time. Sampson was a wonderful part of our family and we will all be together again. As usual, you are here for all of us to show support and compassion. We love you so very much.

Thank you for your friendship,
J., L. and D. Y.

February 16th, 2011

Ken, I hope that the tests ahead for you are easier. Take care, my friend.

D. S.

February 16th, 2011

I love you and am sending you my prayers.

J. F. F.

February 18th, 2011

Ken, I can't even imagine what you are going through, but I feel the pain in your words. I have you and Mickie in my prayers. You are my mentor, friend, and once, you were my boss. You have a great group of people working for you and you are the one who has made them that way. You will always be my dear friend. I have learned a lot from you and will never stop learning from you. Take care, my friend. Love you and Mickie.

K. H.

February 18th, 2011

Ken, you give me such strength reading your journal. I am in such awe and admiration for all that you have gone through, and you still get up each day and smile. *Hugs!*

L. K.

February 21ˢᵗ, 2011

Ken and Mickie, you are both, without a doubt, two of the strongest people I know. Ken, your drive and attitude remind me of a very close friend of mine growing up, that fought his own fight with a terminal beast to the bitter end. J. also continued to work and while others thought he should be home in bed waiting to go. He refused. His passion for his work kept him going strong well beyond what should have been. He continued to teach others and inspire everyone around. I believe he drew his strength from his friends and family, just like you.

I wish you the willingness to continue your fight and hope you never loose the passion and spirit you continue to display. I love you both and I have learned so much from you. You are real heroes to a lot of us. I really do miss my mornings at FLA.

Lots of love and prayers,
B. J. and F. O.

February 23ʳᵈ, 2011

Very well said and oh so true. God bless.

W. G.

February 23ʳᵈ, 2011

I want you to know, my friend, that in life and after you walk through that door, the gifts you give to those of us who know you and you have chosen to share your journey with are immeasurable. Thank you for the gift of wisdom, strength and so much more. It is cherished.

Bless you,
P. F.

February 23rd, 2011

Dear Ken, you are just too awesome! In your struggle to battle the beast, you continue to offer such strength and hope to all those who travel with you on this journey. You are a wonderful teacher and a class act. You remain in my prayers daily and so often in my thoughts.

Blessings to you and Mickie.

Love,
S. and J. W.

February 23rd, 2011

Hang in there, Ken. We love you and pray for you each night and day.

K. and E. K.

February 23rd, 2011

Ken, as I visit Israel and marvel at the things that my people have overcome, I am constantly reminded of you and your strength and grace as you fight the beast. Today as I conclude my visit to this amazing land, I will make sure to add your name, as I frequently do, to the prayers for peace and hope.

L. R. T.

February 24th, 2011

Wishing you a bit of comfort and pain relief, if only for a few moments. I think one cookie would take your mind off the ills of life and give you another five minutes of living it up.

Lots of love and prayers!

Love,
B. J. O.

February 24ᵗʰ, 2011

We love you!

L., J. and D. Y.

February 24ᵗʰ, 2011

Ken, as a fellow health-care provider, your words are inspiring. Keep up the good fight. We all think of you often.

L. (D.) B.

February 26ᵗʰ, 2011

Thank you for sharing your story. God bless you and keep you. You are in our prayers.

J. and J. S. (B.'s mom and stepdad) B. C.

March 14ᵗʰ, 2011

Ken, we think of you and pray for you every day. I just wanted to send you a note to remind you of that and that we are just a call away. Thank you for all you do for everyone.

Love,
T. and S. K.

March 14th, 2011

Hey Ken, I haven't written in a while. As I sit here in the office doing QA (quality assurance), I am reminded of all the lessons you taught me and continue to teach me. While I was thinking of that, a song I'm sure you've heard before came on:

> *He said I was in my early forties, with a lot of life before me. And one moment came that stopped me on a dime, I spent most of the next days, looking at the x-rays, talking 'bout the options and talking 'bout sweet times. I asked him, when it sank in, that this might really be the real end, how's it hit 'cha when you get that kind of news? Man, what do you do? He said:*
>
> *I went skydiving, I went Rocky Mountain climbing, I went two point seven seconds on a bull named Fu Man Chu. And I loved deeper, and I spoke sweeter, and I gave forgiveness I'd been denying, and he said some day I hope you get the chance to live like you were dying.*
>
> *He said I was finally the husband, that most of the time I wasn't. And I became a friend, a friend would like to have. And all of a sudden going fishing wasn't such an imposition. And I went three times that year I lost my dad. Well, I finally read the Good Book and I took a good long hard look, at what I'd do if I could do it all again. And then—(refrain)*
>
> *Like tomorrow was the end, and ya' got eternity to think about what to do with it. What should you do with it, what can I do with it, what would I do with it? (refrain)*

Your resolve, passion, dedication and commitment to not be beaten and to keep pressing forward are forever an inspiration. I try to live each day a little better from your teaching and your examples. Carpe diem, Sir!

J. H.

March 24ᵗʰ, 2011

I love you, Ken Kelly.

R. T.

March 24ᵗʰ, 2011

Thank you. I have been following your journey on this site. I find your journals full of wisdom and very inspiring. I've been wanting to write for quite some time, but just can't seem to find the right words. Nevertheless, I wanted to thank you for sharing your thoughts with all of us. You are in my prayers. PS We miss you at VFVAC.

J. B.

March 24ᵗʰ, 2011

Ken, you will always be remembered long after you leave this world. I remember the first time I met you, some seventeen years ago. You were the instructor in an ILS (intermediate life support) course I was taking. I remember you standing in front of the class and talking, all the while inserting an IV (intravenous) catheter into your own arm and not missing a beat. As a new EMT, I had never seen someone do that. Still, today, I remember that moment every time I start an IV. So yes, Ken, you will *always* be remembered.

W. G.

March 24th, 2011

Ken, be assured you will be remembered. I consider you a friend and a mentor. I thank you for the reminder to always tell those around us what they mean to us. I love you and Mickie, not just for what I learned from you both, but for who you are, what you do and your openness and sharing this fight and journey with the rest of us. Always the teacher, always learning—my life is enriched by knowing you both.

God bless,
P. F.

April 15th, 2011

Mr. Kelly, I have lost one person close to me to cancer and now another is in serious condition with cancer. This is so hard to go through knowing all I know about this disease. What do I tell these people's families? It is so hard. I give you so much credit for your high spirits and always smiling. I hope you are well.

L. K.

April 30th, 2011

Ken, keep the faith and continue to believe! My thoughts are with you and Mickie.

L. (D.) B

April 30th, 2011

God bless you, my friend!

D. Y.

April 30ᵗʰ, 2011

Great news to hear! You continue to amaze me with your strength and courage. Continue on with your journey knowing that those who love and care for you, continue to support you in your battle with the beast.

R. T.

April 30ᵗʰ, 2011

Dearest Ken, praise the Lord for His wonderful blessings. He has answered all of our prayers because He still has work for you to do. You have been such an inspiration to all who know you and love you.

I read your journal entries and my heart is full of admiration for your strength and your faith. You are an amazing human being, Ken. You and Mickie are always in my prayers. Love to both of you.

S. W.

April 30ᵗʰ, 2011

That is so good! I am happy for you. We will keep praying!

S. P.

April 30ᵗʰ, 2011

I am praying for you. I hope to see you at work or at least hear you on the phone. Happy to hear all went well.

J. D.

May 2nd, 2011

I am with you, not just today but with you every day, my friend.

D. O.

May 2nd, 2011

To hear that your surgery had such a positive outcome was some of the best news to brighten a dreary, rainy day. Keep fighting!

Love,
J., D. and M. B.

May 4th, 2011

Glad your spirits are boosted, Sir! You deserve it. Wishing you lots of love and strength.

B. J. O

May 4th, 2011

Ken, we have been to see you twice now that you have been home. S. and I are truly blessed to see how well you are doing and how well you are getting around. The Lord has truly blessed you during this season. We are believing He will be with you always. Our prayers continue to go up for you and for Mickie as well.

T. K.

May 4th, 2011

Mr. Kelly, just a quick note to let you know I think about you often and you are always in my prayers. I hope everything is going strong for you. If you need anything you know where I can be found these days! Thoughts and prayers.

B. S.

May 6th, 2011

Ken, I wonder if we were up in the hospital in Rochester at the same time? I went in on April 20th and had two-thirds of my right lung removed. I stayed there for nine days. I totally concur with your comments about God. Keep up the good fight.

M. H.

June 28th, 2011

Ken, I am so glad that things are looking better and you are feeling better. You are always in my prayers, and I want the best for you.

E. Z. (Y.)

June 28th, 2011

I, for one, am glad you are back from the depths of the deep. You look good and for that I am very happy. Good to see you back and among all of us.

D. S.

June 28th, 2011

We are still here for you and still praying. Glad to see that the prayers are working. Much love from our home to yours!

Love,
J., D. and M. B.

June 28th, 2011

You are such a mighty warrior, Ken. I read your journals and never cease to be amazed at your strength. You keep up the fight, and we'll all keep the prayers going! Love to you and Mickie.

S. W.

June 29th, 2011

Dear Kenny, I am so sorry to hear of the awful times you have recently experienced with your battle against this awful cancer. You are an amazing man, and I'm awed by your strength that you have come through this latest fight. You are in my thoughts and prayers. I love you, and I'm sending lots of love, energy and prayers of strength your way.

K. L. H.

June 30th, 2011

Hello, Sir! I am so glad that you keep on beating this horrible beast. Take one day at a time, Sir. My thoughts and prayers are with you and the Mrs. every single day. I think about you every few hours of every day! You are such an inspiration to me. I love you guys so *much*! Take care and the good Lord will do the rest.

S. P.

June 30th, 2011

Ken, I have said prayers for you and your family. Stay strong and know that your friends are here for you. You will never be lonely;

you have us. Take care of yourself. You are a strong person to keep fighting this beast that is inside you. We all love and respect you.

K. H.

July 1st, 2011

Well, for those of us who can only pray for you, your family and local support structure, I am grateful to read that you are looking good and have won another round with the beast. Keep the faith, and you and yours are always in my prayers. I have thought much about you lately and miss our candid conversations. Stay strong!

C. C.

July 1st, 2011

We are so privileged to call you our dear friend. We all are breathing a sigh of relief for all that you endured the last few months. You are such a strong man and very much adored. You have such a mighty little warrior as your best friend, D. You two together are awesome. You coming to his kindergarten graduation, his baseball games, his swimming practice, mowing the lawn on the tractor together. These are the moments that shape his life. Hold on to that love that he has for you and draw strength from it. We have a great summer ahead.

We love you,
L., J. and D. Y.

July 10th, 2011

Mr. Kelly, I am so happy to learn that you are still with us. I was worried when I didn't see your regular journal posts.

I wanted to let you know that I passed my New York State Paramedic exam. It took me three tries, but I did it! I wanted to make you proud!

I hope that you have a restful and wonderful summer. You are in my prayers and thoughts daily.

L. K.

July 13th, 2011

Ken, you are in my thoughts and prayers. I believe in angels, and I believe they are with you today and always. Sending you lots of positive thoughts.

S. W.

July 13th, 2011

Hang in there my friend. My prayers are with you.

D. S.

July 17th, 2011

Ken, it was good to see you the other day in Wegman's. In spite of all your body has endured recently, you looked good. I continue to pray for inward strength for you and a touch from Heaven to relieve your physical pain. Stay strong in the power of His might and the victory is to be yours. You are an inspiration to many.

T. H.

July 22nd, 2011

Hi Mr. Ken, thinking of you and sending lots of love! Have I told you lately what an amazing man you are? You rock!

K. Y.

August 21st, 2011

I will be praying for you.

B. H.

August 21st, 2011

"The angel of the Lord encamps around those who fear Him, and He delivers them. Taste and see that the Lord is good; blessed is the man who takes refuge in Him" (Psalm 34:7–8).

May God grant you peace, may He surround you with His presence, may He hold you in His arms and guide the surgeons. I pray His angels surround you and let no shadow come near. Be at peace, my friend.

P. F.

August 21st, 2011

"I will fear no evil, for thou are with me". You are in my thoughts, my heart and my prayers.

Love you Ken,
R. T.

August 21ˢᵗ, 2011

I will continue praying for you, Ken. For God to send His angels to protect you and guide the doctors. Always in my thoughts and prayers.

E. Z. (Y.)

August 21ˢᵗ, 2011

Ken, you are in K. and my prayers. The shadow, while always present, will be at bay by the grace of God. God will protect and guide you through this as He always had. We all know that when God wants us, He will call us home and that He will protect us. Remember there are many people that care and will be praying for you. Good luck tomorrow, my friend, and I look forward to talking with you once you return to work.

P. H.

August 21ˢᵗ, 2011

"He alone is my rock and my salvation, He is my fortress, I will never be shaken" (Psalm 62:2). In the worst, most terrifying time in my life, I would repeat this Psalm to myself over and over again. It would, and still does, bring me peace. I hope it does the same for you!
May God's hand stay firmly on your shoulder tomorrow and bless you every second! God bless you, Sir!

C. H.

August 21ˢᵗ, 2011

Ken, I read your message tonight and immediately prayed for you. We will continue to do so tomorrow. So very proud of you and honored to not only know you, but to continue to share in your journey.

A. D.

August 21st, 2011

Dear Kenny, I am praying so very hard for you that you come through this okay. I know God is listening because He has proved it to me over and over these few weeks. You are in my heart and soul. God bless you and take care of you. No matter what, you will be cradled in His arms and the light of the angels. I love you and am sending lots of love and prayers for your healing your way. God bless you!

Your cuz, K. L. H.

August 21st, 2011

Dearest Ken, God will be watching over you as He has always been. You will be in my prayers and thoughts. Sending love to you and Mickie.

S. W.

August 21st, 2011

We will be praying for you.

S. P.

August 22nd, 2011

Dearest Ken, I am sorry you are struggling with this shadow and fear. I will hold you in my heart and ask that you come through this with the strength and will you have before. Do your best to keep the negativity out of your mind and consciousness. Negativity only feeds the shadow. You fought it off while you sat in the chair and you can continue to fight it off through this test. Then, when the time comes, you will not be in the arms of fear but embraced in love and peace. Take your power back so the decision can be yours. Good luck!

L. B.

August 22nd, 2011

Ken, my thoughts and prayers are with you this morning. May the angels watch over you and keep you safe.

L. (D.) B.

August 22nd, 2011

Ken, we are praying for you, my friend. Stay positive and may the angels always be with you.

B. and R. G.

August 22nd, 2011

I said a prayer for you today, Ken, that God will send the angel you asked for. He will do it, and He will be there for you during this time. Remember what God says to us, *"When you saw one set of footprints, it was then that I carried you".*

K. N. B.

August 22nd, 2011

Mr. Kelly, I pray you will be comforted during the operation and recovery.

L. K.

August 22nd, 2011

I believe we deal every day with the natural world and most forget that the spiritual world is actually the real world! But remember, dear friend, life and death are in the power of the tongue! I speak out loud at this time and tell the shadow to cease and for God's angels to stand guard over you! Yea, though you walk through the valley of the shadow of death, you will fear no evil! God's rod and staff will comfort you! Amen.

D. T.

August 22nd, 2011

Our dearest Ken, this shadow is not ready for you yet. This shadow is finding that your strength is much stronger with the angels who have been watching over you and all the prayers for you are keeping this shadow at bay. You have proven that your faith and strength to fight this beast is a very powerful one. We all who know you pray more than once a day for you and love you very much. Please be strong as we know you will be. This is just yet another test. A test you will get through. We love you!

K. and E. K.

August 23rd, 2011

Uncle Ken, what good news to hear your surgery went well and you were home the same day. Now the shadow had diminished! You are not ready for the shadow and the shadow senses that. I believe in angels and I believe you have many around you, both physical and nonphysical. Our thoughts and prayers are with you every day.

Wishing you an uneventful and speedy recovery so you can enjoy this weather that you love so much.

All our love,
R., A., A. and T. B.

August 23rd, 2011

I loved hearing this, I had way too many losses this last month or so. I don't think I could deal with another one right now. Will continue to keep you in my thoughts and prayers. They tell me God won't give me anything I can't handle or too much to handle at once, so this is my proof. I am truly excited you made it through this surgery and are on another road to recovery.

B. H.

August 23rd, 2011

What an amazing praise! Thank you for sharing this with us. It brings hope not only to you, but to others! Goodbye shadow. The light has spread!

D. T.

August 23rd, 2011

Great job, Ken! I'm so happy to hear the good news. Wishing you a speedy recovery and a bike ride soon!

L. B.

August 24ᵗʰ, 2011

Awesome job!

Love,
J. D. and M. B.

August 24ᵗʰ, 2011

We will always be there to support you. We will always be there in prayer.

We love you, Ken.
K. and E. K.

August 24ᵗʰ, 2011

Way to go, Ken. Kick its butt!

D. S.

August 24ᵗʰ, 2011

Dearest Ken, you are living proof that prayers are real and answered. I pray for your comfort, healing and that the beautiful white light of God and your angel guides continue to surround and protect you. I'm so glad you came through this surgery safe and sound. The tests you and your body are going through are awful, and I'm sad that you have to endure them. You continue to be an amazing inspiration to all of us who love you and care about you. You're always in my thoughts and prayers.

K. L. H.

August 24th, 2011

K. and I are so glad to hear that you are doing well. We look forward to seeing you soon.

P. H.

August 25th, 2011

Hi Kenny, as always, I think of you with love. Glad you got to August 23rd with a lightening of the load. I love you.

J. F. F.

September 12th, 2011

The physical infirmities you face can never overshadow the man that you are. It's a terrible thing you are enduring, but your courage and openness is helping others in ways probably no one can realize.

God will hold you! He will let you know when it is time to fight on and when it is time to rest. I pray He spares you from much more pain and fog and gives you the strength and peace to carry on. Remember, the shadow is just that, a shadow. It was defeated on the cross and can only remain a shadow.

P. F.

September 12th, 2011

Ken, my heart aches to hear all you are going through. We, your family, friends and coworkers, would never see you as a weak person. You are strong in so many ways. We are all here for you, whether it is to watch you walk or we carry you taking care of your yard. That is what family and friends do for each other. We all love you so much and care about how you are. We really do want to help. You just have to let us do it. You have given to so many people over the years, but you don't like people giving or caring for you because you think it makes you look weak. Sometime you have to let people use their gifts that God gave them also. Remember, that shadow can't do anything God doesn't want it to do. You are in His hands.

Praying for you and Mickie always. You have never been, and will never be, a burden to your family and friends, ever.

T. K.

September 12th, 2011

Dear Ken, I am so saddened by your troubles. You are forever in my prayers and in my thoughts. I believe that when we have learned all that we need to learn and taught all that we need to teach, our Heavenly Father takes us home. You still have work to do. Ken, you are such a caring, loving and giving individual. You will always be remembered for those gifts as well as the strong, dedicated man that you are right now. You have touched so many lives and made such a difference for so many people. God has blessed us with your friendship. Stay strong and know that you are loved by so many.

S. W.

September 12th, 2011

Ken-Ken, you are strong and courageous. I believe in you. We all do.

C. T.

September 12th, 2011

Ken, the shadow shall be defeated, as it was on that fateful day on the cross. God is with you and your family. He gives you strength and courage. You, my friend, have waged a heroic battle against this beast; and the beast can never break who you are. You have given of yourself to mankind and have made a great difference in the lives of many.

As your battle continues, remember, my friend, that we are with you. When you are scared, lean on us, and we will carry you through. There are many people who care and love you, and it is time that you let us carry you through these difficult times.

You are always in K.'s and my prayers. We pray for comfort. We pray that He will give strength to you and your family. Stay strong, and remember that we are here for you.

P. H.

September 12ᵗʰ, 2011

Ken, I cried when I read your words. You are my dearest friend, bowling partner, crew chief, and boss. Your words of wisdom will be with me always. I love you and Mickie dearly and always will. Be strong. You are in my prayers.

Love,
K. H.

September 12ᵗʰ, 2011

Mr. Kelly, I have been reading your posts for some time now, and they always pull me in two different directions. I'm saddened for what you have had to deal with, but then I'm proud for the way you insist on not giving up. Sir, you are an inspiration to everyone you meet, including myself and all your other employees, past and present. Sir, my prayers have, and always will, go out for you and Mickie.

B. S.

September 12th, 2011

Ken, you are such a pillar of faith, of strength and of courage. I remember last year, before my brain surgery, thinking that I wished I had all of your qualities. I also remember saying repeatedly that God doesn't give us more than we can handle and God knows how strong you are. You have the love, respect faith and courage of all of us behind you. Stay strong, my friend. You are in my prayers. I think that I will refer to you as Ken the Warrior because that is what you are. You humble me, Mr. Kelly. XO.

B. B.

September 12th, 2011

Mr. Kelly, my thoughts are with you at this time.

L. K.

September 12th, 2011

Ken, I thought about you today and then I saw your post. Always know that you have touched the lives of thousands. Carry on, Ken!

L. (D.) B.

September 14th, 2011

Prayers and love to you.

J. B.

September 14ʰ, 2011

Hello, my dear sweet Ken. You and I have talked many, many times about those shadows and the fear that they cause you. I can only imagine. I can only imagine the pain that you feel. I wish I could take those fears and that pain from you. What I can do is be present. You and I speak or connect in some way each and every day. We have a friendship that is true. Please know I am always here for you and that I love you with all my heart. The battle you fight is awful, but you have a million supporters. You are in our prayers. You are D.'s number one best friend. The Great Uncle Ken! He worships you, and his love never wavers. You teach him a great many lessons. Most especially about life, lemons and lemonade! That was a great time last weekend when you and he made the lemonade cookie stand. You are awesome. I don't think I'll get my orthopedic surgeon after all—it's sales from now on, I do believe!

Keep your chin up,
L. M. Y.

September 16ʰ, 2011

My dearest Kenly! We have not spoken in some time, but let it be known that I love and miss you and Mickie terribly. I have always looked to you as one of my idols. I feel that you can conquer this beast within. For you, Ken, are my hero.

Love you,
H. K.

September 22ⁿᵈ, 2011

I agree with you, Ken. We can learn from all of our experiences. No experience is useless. Everyone has a lesson. We can choose to learn from it or ignore it. The beast may thrive on our imperfections, our limitations and all. But it can't stifle our potential, unless we choose to. I have always liked the adage, *"Life is God's gift to you. What you do with your life is your gift to God"*.

E. Z. (Y.)

September 22nd, 2011

Ken, it was nice to see you the other night. It gives me hope and inspiration when I read your comments, knowing you can stay so strong and positive during your fight. Stay strong, my friend.

B. G.

September 22nd, 2011

Dear Ken, you are such an awesome human being! Through all that you have suffered through, you continue to inspire us all. And that little guy in the photo with you surely helps you to keep pushing on.

Love you, Ken and Mickie. Enjoy your trip.

S. W.

September 22nd, 2011

Mankind is better.

D. S.

September 22nd, 2011

There is the Ken Kelly I know! You have found the purpose in this and are going to help others find that purpose too. You have found a positive spin, and that will keep you uplifted. Keep holding on to that, Ken, and so will we. I will pray for you, for Mickie and the doctors who are treating you. You are not alone. With all this support behind you, we'll send the shadow off to bother someone else!

K. N. B.

September 22ⁿᵈ, 2011

Welcome back to your life, Ken! For your information, you're amazing and always have been. Good to know you are back!

L. B.

September 23ʳᵈ, 2011

Ken, I just read your September 22ⁿᵈ post. You have been in my prayers daily. I'm so glad that you have turned up your positive attitude on us. We need your influence, maybe not today, but when we least expect it, perhaps someday for a loved one or ourselves. Your penning is absolutely profound and something I can understand. With Shakespeare, I needed an interpreter. Please keep coming at us!

Thanks,
J. K.

September 25ᵗʰ, 2011

In honor of Ken Kelly!

M. D.

September 27ᵗʰ, 2011

Dearest Kenny, I am so sorry for the pain. I know that you suffer, yet you always find the light at the end of the dark night. I think of you many times a day and always send a prayer and lots of love.

I hope Jamaica has been very joyful for you in spite of your pain.

Lots of love,
J. F. F.

November 15th, 2011

There are times when the words I want to say just aren't there. This is one of those times. Very poignant and beautifully written. I think of you daily and cherish the brief conversations we have on the rare occasions we see each other at work. I sent you, at least in my mind, a prayer for healing as you walk away from me and hope that you can feel it. One of those mysteries of our lives, the gifts we give and wonder if they are felt. Really a deep thought there! Your family and your friends will continue to care for you always, to love you and to pray for you. Thank you for sharing.

R. T.

November 15th, 2011

Ken, your words give me some comfort, knowing that you saw your mother and brother in your dream. I didn't know your brother, but I did know your mother, and she was like a mother to me and many others in the EMS world. She was a grandmother to my kids. Cherish those dreams because I know that you have comfort in them. My prayers are with you and your family. You are like a big brother to me. I will always remember the good times we shared.

Keep the fight up on this beast as I know you have the strength to do so. It was really great seeing you the other day in Wegman's. Take care of yourself and Mickie.

K. H.

November 15ᵗʰ, 2011

Hello Ken, it has been a while since I wrote. I tend to suspect it was more than a dream that you described today. What a wonderful chance to see your family again. I have "dreamed" of my uncle and my father many times. I have always thought of it as a form of communication rather than just a dream.

Thinking of you and Mickie.

B. S.

November 15ᵗʰ, 2011

Dearest Ken, you simply take my breath away and leave me speechless. Stay strong, dear friend. Love to you and Mickie.

S. and J. W.

November 15ᵗʰ, 2011

Ken, I am glad to hear you are still working. EMS will never be the same when you stop working, no matter the reason. Our thoughts and prayers are with you always.

W. G.

November 15ᵗʰ, 2011

Uncle Ken, you continue to amaze and inspire me. I am so glad you were able to have some fun during these last months with the recent trips you have made, despite what you are battling.

Thank you for sharing your most personal thoughts with us, regardless if they are up or down moments. They help us understand this "beast" in a more personal way. Even if we have had a close personal, friend or family experience, the more we know and learn about how this beast effects each experience, the better defenses we have to battle it. Only a strong person is able to share what you have shared with us, so don't apologize for sharing. What you are really doing is teaching us and arming us with the tools we need for the future. I personally thank you for giving that to me.

Your dream brought tears to my eyes. My favorite color has always been green, and when you stated my father was painting his room *green*, of all colors, had special meaning, kind of ironic. I have always thought of green as a sign of life. In the spring, green signals life is renewing. Summer, all is green and alive. In the fall, when the green fades, the evergreens stay strong, even through the winter, as a reminder that a renewal is right around the corner. Always something to look forward to.

Grandma was always the person to go to if you needed comfort and peace. She was the foundation to what we all are. The yellow paint not sticking in your room is a sign that you are not done. The yellow is the "beast" and you're not ready to have it "stick".

Grandma and Dad were sending you a message that when we get to the point we are all destined to, there is life, comfort and peace waiting, when it's time, when God says it's time.

That's my interpretation anyway. Take it or leave it. Each person's dream is specific to them, but thank you for sharing *this* one. Thank you for sharing this one with me.

I love you. I pray for you and I think of you each day.

A. B.

November 15th, 2011

Tears, prayers and love for you! Thank you for sharing the truth even though the beast is fighting you every step of the way. It is good for all of us to know how it is challenging you so we can know how to pray effectively. Love from Washington State!

D. T.

November 16th, 2011

I will continue to pray for you, Ken. If you need anything, just let me know.

E. Z. (Y.)

November 16th, 2011

Ken, I love you Sir and thank you for sharing such a personal moment with all of us. You help keep us strong even though I feel I should be delivering some magical cookies to your door! Keep fighting your fight.

Love,
F. and B. J. O.

November 18th, 2011

Thinking of you, Ken.

D. S.

November 18th, 2011

This Thanksgiving I am thankful for a lot of things. To be able to still tell you Happy Thanksgiving as well has more meaning to me that you will ever know. Much love to you and your family as the holiday season starts.

J. B.

December 12th, 2011

In honor of Ken Kelly. God bless you on this journey. You have been and are an awesome love and teacher to us all who love. Give my love to all!

K. L. H.

February 10th, 2012

Ken, you are such a source of strength, persistence and tenacity that I admire. If you ever need someone to just type for you, I'd be glad to help. You are and have been in my prayers daily.

J. K.

February 10th, 2012

We are still praying for you.

S. P.

February 10th, 2012

Ken, your spirit and strength in this fight is such an inspiration. We will continue to keep you in our prayers.

K. D.

February 10th, 2012

Dear Ken, I am so saddened by all the pain and suffering you have had to endure because of the wretched "beast". I am so amazed by your strength of spirit through all of this. I am so grateful that your faith in our Heavenly Father sustains you along with your family and devoted friends. You are truly a gift to all who know you. You and Mickie are in my thoughts and prayers.

Love to you both,
S. and J. W.

February 10th, 2012

You are an amazing man with a strong will. You amaze me every day. You are such an inspiration to me. I am so thankful that God put you in my life. Sending lots of hugs and love to you.

L. C.

February 10th, 2012

Ken, I am so grateful to know you. You are a very special person with a strength that is amazing as well as inspirational. All our thoughts and prayers are with you and Mickie. Keep fighting and make the angels even stronger. God bless and keep you strong.

M. and D. B.

February 10th, 2012

Ken, when I think I'm tired, I think of your unfailing vim and vigor and move on. When I am in pain, I think of your strength in the midst of your pain. When I am feeling down, I look at how fortunate I am to have you as a friend and boss. I still remember the day I came to Finger Lakes Ambulance for my interview. You embraced me in spite of my faults.

I pray that I can be even half the person you are. Thank you, my dear friend, and say hi to Mickie for me! Love and kisses to you two!

D. T.

February 10th, 2012

Our prayers continue to go out to you. You are an amazing man. You are loved by many people, who have learned so much from you and in so many ways. Blessings to you!

L. O.

February 11th, 2012

Ken, you are an amazing man. Every day that I think my pain and limited mobility are taking the best of me, I think of you and the hard time that you are going through, and it seems to push me on. Thank you for being such an inspiration. You truly are a wonderful person, father, uncle and, most of all, a *true friend*. My thoughts and prayers are with you and Mickie. I love you both so very much.

D. P.

February 12th, 2012

You are in my constant thoughts and prayers, Kenny. I love you. B. sends his love too.

J. F. F.

February 12th, 2012

Dear Ken, I will say even extra prayers for you so that you can push the beast back. Your faith and strong will are amazing. Best wishes.

B. S.

February 12ᵗʰ, 2012

Extra hugs and prayers coming your way! Love to you and Mickie.

K. Y.

February 17ᵗʰ, 2012

Still by your side from afar, sending love and support. You are truly an inspiration!

Love you all,
J., D. and M. B.

February 17ᵗʰ, 2012

Carpe diem, Ken! Today I have decided, like you, to think of others rather than myself and the misery of a divorce. I have a wonderful eleven-year-old son, great friends and family. God bless and thanks for sharing your strength with us who need a little lift in life sometimes.

B. S.

February 17ᵗʰ, 2012

Always good to hear positive news. Stay healthy and positive.

J. D.

February 17ᵗʰ, 2012

Our dearest Ken, you do not have to feel guilty of your feelings of life and especially of the beast. It is okay to feel glum. It is okay to feel angry. It is okay to hate (the beast). It is okay for you to cry.

We all cry with you. It is okay to feel happy. It is okay to love, laugh, sing, cry, scream and smile. Guilt is not anything you should feel. Please don't. We know this is difficult for you because of the person you are. The guilt you feel is because of your love for life and human beings and what has stricken others that are suffering. Just know we all love you and are here for you at any time. You are in our hearts and prayers always. We love you.

K. and E. K.

February 17th, 2012

Good to hear that today is better and we all have days that are rough as you said. The outcome of those rough days is all in how we choose to handle them. Love from all of us.

J. B.

February 17th, 2012

Ken, in all the years I have known you, you have always made it a point to teach. Even now I find great lessons of life from your words.

It was great seeing you the other day. K. and I keep learning about strength, love and life with each post. God be with you and yours.

P. H.

February 17th, 2012

Glad to hear things are starting to look up. I think about you every day when I wake up and in pain. I think that my pain is nothing compared to yours. You really are my hero and I look up to you very much. I hope we can be there for each other. I would *love* to hear from you when you need someone to talk to, no matter the time of day. If you just can't sleep and are in so much pain, *please* just give me a ring, and we can talk.

I have found that going through all that I have been with loosing my leg, etc., that is *a lot* easier to talk to someone else who is also going through a troubled time. *I am here for you, Sir, day or night!* I hope to hear from you very soon, at least a phone call to chat.

Thank you, Sir, and I hope you start feeling better. My thoughts and prayers are with you and Mickie. I love you both very much.

D. P.

February 17th, 2012

Ken, you are truly an inspiration. Prayers are with you, my friend.

D. S.

February 17th, 2012

We love you, Ken. Just keep up the fight. We will keep sending the prayers.

Love,
M. and D. B.

February 18th, 2012

It's inspiring to read your words, Ken. You have such a gift with them. Your fighting spirit is amazing. Love you!

L. B.

February 20th, 2012

Ken, you are remarkable! I don't think I could do what you have done and are doing now. You are always in my thoughts.

J. L.

February 28th, 2012

In honor of Ken Kelly. Your courage is contagious and helps us all stand taller knowing you. An admirer.

Anonymous

March 6th, 2012

Ken, again you truly amaze us all. Your strength in deed and words are truly what helps us as much as it helps you. Thank you again for helping me smile again.

T. K.

March 23rd, 2012

Ken, I am so glad you are listening to the birds singing. It is something I don't take for granted as many others do. Give a *huge hug* to Mickie for me and a big hug to yourself as well.

Be well,
R. S.

March 23rd, 2012

Hello, Sir. I am glad to hear that you are enjoying the sounds of the birds and the beautiful outdoors. You inspire me every day. I wake up and think about you. You keep me wanting to fight to walk again.

I too recently went to the doctors and ended up having to go to Geneva General Hospital for an Ultrasound. They say I have an AAA (abdominal aortic aneurysm) in the abdomen, which I knew about, that is only 3.3 centimeters. What I did not know, that I found out about, was that I also have an aneurysm and dissection of the aortic arch that is about 4.5 cm. It also runs into the carotid artery, which is now dissected.

I think about all that you are going through and read about how you enjoy every day and live life to the fullest and that makes me want to fight harder. You are my *hero*. I am, and *always* will be, here for you and Mickie if you guys ever need anything. I would love to get together with you both one day if you have time, even if it's just sitting in a living room and chatting.

May God watch over you and *bless* you each and every day. We both have guardian angels looking down on us, protecting us. *I love you both so very much.*

D. P.

March 23rd, 2012

Ken, you never cease to amaze me. Thank you for making me stop and smell the roses! Have a wonderful time in San Diego. It is such a beautiful city. Love to you and Mickie.

S. W.

March 24th, 2012

Ken, I am not sure if you got my latest. My CT (computed tomography) scan showed shadows, which the radiation doctor couldn't tell if the tumor had come back or if it was scar tissue. Off I went to another PET (positron emission tomography) scan, which came back as scar tissue.

Yes, I enjoy your journal as you are indeed a master writer, among other things. I continue to pray for you on a daily basis as I say my rosary with my wife and dogs. Take care.

M. H.

March 24ᵗʰ, 2012

Amen!

D. T.

March 29ᵗʰ, 2012

Mr. Kelly, you are an amazing man. Good luck with your trip and upcoming battle with the beast. You have a great support system behind you, Sir.

L. K.

April 16ᵗʰ, 2012

You continue to motivate all who love and care for you. Enjoy your vacation and know you are being upheld. Love you, Ken.

R. T.

April 16ᵗʰ, 2012

Congrats, Ken! I'm glad that you intend to be around a long time. My prayers for you and yours are being answered. Keep up the great work, Kid!

J. K.

April 16ᵗʰ, 2012

I enjoy reading your journal. It not only keeps me in touch with your journey; it also enlightens me and makes me reflect on myself.

With great admiration and respect,
Your student E. A.

April 17ᵗʰ, 2012

Beautiful and inspirational! We love you and know you are a fighter.

Love,
K. and E. K.

April 17ᵗʰ, 2012

God bless you, Ken. You are an amazing man and on an amazing journey. You sharing what is happening is a lesson to us all. I love you and hang in there!

Love,
K. L. H.

April 22ⁿᵈ, 2012

Stay strong. You are an inspiration to all of us.

Love,
J., D. and M. B.

June 29th, 2012

Pulling for you, Ken. You are an inspiration as always.

D. S.

June 29th, 2012

You are my inspiration. If it wasn't for you, I don't know how I would handle the cards we have just been dealt. Our prayers and love.

M. and D. B.

June 29th, 2012

My friend Ken, I am so glad to hear that you are feeling better. The good days are nice. As I read through your journal, the wisdom, courage and strength you demonstrate is remarkable. I have lost several friends who were younger than you and they just gave up. You are a light through all of this darkness and you remind me never to give up hope. The number of lives that you have touched is probably uncountable. The way you have changed the course of human history is, as of yet, unknown. You are a teacher, a healer and a family man. You are a manager, yes, but not your first calling, Ken. You and I both know you would prefer to be in the trenches helping people rather than sitting "up on the hill".

So as these days go on and you have a hard time remembering things while in a meeting, so what. We all care about you and love you. We all are there for you and your family. All you need to do is ask, and it will be done.

Here is to praying that you have a fantastic summer and are able to do the things that make you happy. If you are going to ride, let me know because it would be an honor to ride with you, Sir. K. would be thrilled to ride with you also. Heck, I will even deck my bike hour for the ride.

Take care, my friend, and may God bless you and your family with His love and comfort.

Your friend,
P. H.

June 29th, 2012

Ken, it's hard to express my thoughts into words. However, what I can say is that you are truly an amazing person. In your times of despair, you keep the faith and notice others worse off. You continue to work despite the pain. You don't complain about the hand you were dealt, but instead, you teach others and prove to us all that you are a remarkable man that we are all blessed to know.

Paraphrased and changed tense of 2 Timothy 4:7; I "continue" to fight, I "am running" the race and I "am keeping" the faith.

J. B.

June 29th, 2012

Hi Ken, it was great to see you in Walmart a week or two ago. You looked wonderful, and I hope you and Mickie are having a great summer. Keep fighting the beast, and I will keep you in my prayers.

B. S.

June 30th, 2012

Ken, thank you again for the updates. You have, and will, live in many, many people's lives and memories forever. You have touched so many people in the past three years with this beast. *But* even before this, you had already been a part of so many people's lives. I just couldn't tell you the numbers even if I had the time to do so. You stay strong, and when you can't, call one of us, and we will carry you. God bless you!

T. K.

June 30th, 2012

In honor of Ken Kelly, a man that I wish I could be. A leader, a healer, a brave and courageous man.

P. H.

June 30th, 2012

Ken, your strength and words of wisdom never cease to amaze me. You are truly an inspiration to all. My prayers are out to you, your family and the huge extended family you have in the EMS community. I miss working for you and don't seem to have the opportunity to stop in just to say *hi*, so here I am saying *hi* and thinking of you.

E. A.

July 1st, 2012

Ken, congrats on your surgery success! I've been concerned about you from the first week of May and prayed that things were going well for you! I enjoy your writings. They are an inspiration to me and how I should be living my own life, which has no complications. I'm glad you have a new lease on life. You deserve it, man! I hope that you can enjoy the summer more now! Take care and continue to stay strong!

J. K.

July 4th, 2012

Ken, you know you are loved, and that is the most powerful medicine of all. You are still on my prayer list and prayed for twice a day by myself and K. I don't know if anyone told you, but M. F., an EMT in Dundee, eighty-one-year-old, died last week. She was a good one. See you at the next meeting.

M. H.

July 6th, 2012

Wow, I'm not even sure I can put into words how inspiring reading your journal entries are. I have been through many struggles, and continue to go through them, and often get mad at myself for still struggling. But focusing on the struggle doesn't help. It's focusing on overcoming the painful situations that are thrown into my life. I had oftentimes blamed myself for my struggles, seeming so insignificant when there are so many others in this world who hurt way more than myself and are fighting *much* bigger beasts. I see you say the same thing, and it fills me with hope because I feel my struggles are nothing compared to yours.

What an amazing heart you have for people. I can hope to have the same courage and endurance as you. Your writing is tremendous. It has really touched me. It takes *so* much strength to be honest and open about struggles. Your brutal honesty about things, which could be embarrassing, is so completely impressive. I know that I don't know you well, but please know that you have forever impacted yet another life. I know you have already touched so many people's lives.

Thank you for your encouraging words. Thank you for putting the desire in my heart to fight even harder for my dreams and my passions. I have always said that if by sharing my struggles, I can help but one person, then all the pain and hardship I have suffered is all worth it. Thank you for your inspiration.

D. W.

October 31st, 2012

Stay strong, my friend. My prayers are with you.

W. G.

October 31st, 2012

Hi, Ken, you remain in my thoughts and prayers. I am in awe at your strength and openness through your battle with this beast. I have always thought of you as a teacher and mentor. The life lessons you are giving me right now are incomparable.

Blessings to both you and your lovely wife. I will be visiting one of your dispatchers in a few weeks. If you are free for lunch, I'm buying.

In Him,
P. F.

October 31st, 2012

Dearest Ken, you are in my thoughts and prayers every day. My heart is sad, but I rejoice in the fact that you continue to fight this horrible beast. You are a truly remarkable man. I pray that God will lessen your pain. I pray that yet through faith in Him, He will continue to give you the strength you need to get through each day.

My love to you and Mickie.

S. and J. W.

October 31st, 2012

The Armor of God:

"Finally, be strong in the Lord and in His mighty power. Put on the full armor of God, so that you can take your stand against the devil's schemes. For our struggle is not against flesh and blood, but against the

275

rulers, against the authorities, against the powers of this dark world and against the spiritual forces of evil in the Heavenly realms. Therefore, put on the full armor of God, so that when the day of evil comes, you may be able to stand your ground, and after you have done everything, to stand. Stand firm then, with the belt of truth buckled around your waist, with the breastplate of righteousness in place, and with your feet fitted with the readiness that comes from the gospel of peace. In addition to all this, take up the shield of faith, with which you can extinguish all the flaming arrows of the evil one. Take the helmet of salvation and the sword of the Spirit, which is the word of God. And pray in the Spirit on all occasions with all kinds of prayers and requests. With this in mind, be alert and always keep on praying for all the Lord's people" (Ephesians 6:10–18).

I just thought you needed a few inspiring words. Keep the faith and continue the fight. Your friends and family are here for you.

J. B.

October 31ˢᵗ, 2012

Ken, my friend, teacher, boss and mentor. How I wish you were not going through this journey. You deserve so much better. You are strong, but I am afraid you are tired, my friend. Lean on your friends and loved ones. We will carry you forward to whatever the future may bring.

Please know you are not alone. K. and I are only a phone call away. We are here for you and your family, Ken. I don't care if it is taking you to a doctor's appointment or grocery shopping, just ask.

We have seen much together and as always, I am available to you. You have done so much for me, and like you always said, I tried to pay it forward. Rest easy in His arms, and know that we are here for you.

P. H.

October 31ˢᵗ, 2012

Ken-Ken, you are in my thoughts. I continue to admire your strength, your wisdom and your courage. Please continue to share the burdens and the triumphs. We, the many who are indebted to for your years of selfless service, are listening and praying.

C. T.

October 31ˢᵗ, 2012

I am truly amazed at your strength and determination. Love surrounds you daily. We pray for you, we understand when you're having a bad day, and we hurt when we see you hurt. I thank God every day for blessing me with you in my life. You have watched me grow from twenty years old to now thirty-five. You have witnessed me becoming a mother and so many other milestones. I thank you for being a part of me and teaching me the meaning of life. You are my hero and a true inspiration. I love you, Ken.

L. C.

October 31ˢᵗ, 2012

Mr. Kelly, please enjoy your vacation. I hope you feel better soon. My thoughts and prayers are with you always.

L. K.

October 31ˢᵗ, 2012

Remember, your friends think of you all the time. I will be back in town this weekend, so if you want to have lunch (even if it is a small one), come on Tuesday to Geneva. D. and I will take you out to lunch.

J. D.

October 31ˢᵗ, 2012

Ken, I wish I had the wisdom to offer words to help make your journey easier. Know that you are not alone, ever! I am sure there are many, many people that you are unaware of that hold you in their thoughts and prayers. May God bless.

C. H.

November 1ˢᵗ, 2012

Prayers are with you, my friend.

D. S.

November 1ˢᵗ, 2012

Dearest Ken, your family and friends will never waiver from you. Yes, it is difficult for you to do the things in life you love. This is a setback in the battle you fight with the beast; however, many battles are won in a war after setbacks.

We love you and pray every day for our brother who is so strong and has such a love of life, family and people. We are all here for you to do whatever you need.

We love you.

K. and E. K.

November 1ˢᵗ, 2012

Stay strong, Ken. You are in my prayers every day.

M. H.

November 2nd, 2012

Ken, I'm sorry to hear of your struggle and pain. You are one of the bravest people I know. You continue to do so much with your life, and you haven't let the cancer control you. You have many victories and achievements to celebrate. I hope you can find energy to focus on them too. Love you.

L. B.

November 3rd, 2012

Ken, the kids and I are still praying for strength for you. If you ever want to do lunch, let me know. We would be happy and honored to take you out. Take care.

Love,
J., D. and little M. B.

November 7th, 2012

Ken, while the beast may prevent you from practicing in the streets, you must remember *you* have made the majority of the paramedics in this region, and the entire Upstate Region of New York, the providers that they are. Your hands and knowledge have shaped these men and women into a group of first-class paramedics providing outstanding medical care to the communities.

I will take it a step farther and present you with the fact that you changed the way EMS is delivered to the residents of the Finger Lakes Region, and in fact throughout New York State. One of the first companies in the state to have RSI (rapid sequence intubation). The first organized and trained ERT (emergency response team) groups in the area. You took a small company to a successful EMS provider.

I could only dream to leave a legacy as distinguished and as noble as yours. Long after you are done working, this community owes you a dept that *never* can be repaid. God bless you, Ken, for all that you have done for the area and mankind.

P. H.

November 7ᵗʰ, 2012

Ken, you are a sensei. That is teacher in Japanese and usually referred to as a teacher of karate. He teaches his students the martial arts, not so much for self-defense but for a belief and ability in oneself. I'm a freelance computer teacher. If I show someone how to make their computer work for them and not be a slave of their computer, I have freed them. Sadly, I don't see their creations, nor have much contact afterward. But what a good teacher does is to duplicate one's abilities in others, helping them to achieve their potential, which gives them satisfaction, eventually. You have brought skills and satisfaction to your students, employees and fellow professionals. Nice. Excellent! You have become a mentor, probably without knowing it. I admire you for being both a sensei and mentor. I wish I could become both someday. Hang in there, Guy.

J. K.

November 7ᵗʰ, 2012

Try not to think of loosing a ministry but instead passing on your gifts to hundreds of students to follow in your path of helping others. Now, even more people will be helped and cared for. I just wish I was so lucky as to have been one of those students.

J. B.

November 7ᵗʰ, 2012

Ken, even at this time in your life, you still give life to others. What you have given over the years to others will be continued for years and years after we are all gone from this life here. You have a long list of people you have trained and respect you. Please just take one day at a time and truly enjoy each day. Remember what you have given. Many of us have no list!

T. K.

November 7ᵗʰ, 2012

Dearest Ken, you have made such an incredible contribution to mankind just by your very being. I can't fathom the sadness that is in your heart. But I know the sadness that is in mine for all that you have had to endure to fight the beast. You are an amazing man, an amazing friend and an amazing teacher. How fortunate we all are to know you.

Keeping you in my thoughts and prayers.

S. W.

November 7ᵗʰ, 2012

Ken, you are a true teacher and you will be leaving a great legacy behind, but you are not through yet! I am sure you have even more to give and there are others that are going to still learn from you. I was thinking the other day about a day that you helped me and taught me something. It was the day when we were working at the Shurfine Store and the neighbor boy that lived downstairs from me put his arm through the glass. I was fine taking care of him and got through the emergency, then I started to melt. You said to just stop, breathe deeply and relax. I still do that today and I remember you each time.

You are still a big part of the ambulance and paramedics. I, for one, would like to say thank you so very much.

M. B.

November 19ᵗʰ, 2012

Hi Dear Cousin, I am so sorry for your sorrow. Yet, in facing it, we hone in on the true clarity of the jewel of our lives. One thing I have discovered this past couple of years, everyone asks "Why?" when troubles become overwhelmingly heavy. Yet a wise friend reminded me, there is no answer to "Why?" It just is. At least, I stopped tormenting myself with the search for an answer. I love you.

J. F. F.

March 3ʳᵈ, 2013

Thinking about you!

A. B.

March 25ᵗʰ, 2013

I've just reread your November 7ᵗʰ post and understand where you're coming from. I should be thinking about retiring, but I'm not interested yet. I saw your quote in the *Daily Messenger Newspaper* recently. It was great! I visited with M. and J. M. last week, and we all care.

Continue to write when you can. You're really good at it! If ever I can do anything for you, let me know.

J. K.

April 2ⁿᵈ, 2013

You are so strong. I admire you. Keep up the fight, sir.

L. K.

April 2nd, 2013

Ken, I think of you and pray for you often. Thank you for the honest way in which you bare your soul as you continue on in this fight. You have invested your life as a teacher of many. You will continue to do the same as you teach us all about living victoriously in the face of pain and the death that we all will face one day.

J. D.

April 2nd, 2013

Hi Ken! I've been thinking of you lately. I've figured out a homemade shortbread cookie! As soon as this semester is over, I'll bake a few and head out. You're and inspiration and continue to teach us all. Shout out to Mickie! I miss you so much!

We love you,
F. and B. J.O.

April 2nd, 2013

Ken, I see you often and still am amazed how you have lived the past few years. You have touched our hearts and lives so much. You have shown us all that if you set your mind to a goal, it will be more powerful than any beast. Just remember we are all praying and standing with you. You have to walk this mostly by yourself, but if you need to be carried, we are here for you. Thank you for all the wisdom and strength you have shown us all. May our Lord Jesus continue to give you a long, long life and the strength to hold your ground and help you with the horrible pain you endure each day.

T. and S. K.

April 4th, 2013

Ken, great to read your writings! The one posted on April 2nd is definitely a keeper and worth rereading. Thank you!

J. K.

April 7th, 2013

A big hug for you, Sir.

D. O.

July 10th, 2013

I know that God is with you every step you take. Your work on this earth is not yet complete. So He inspires you with sunshine, the sweet sounds of birds singing, the smell of freshly mown grass, a summer rainstorm and on and on. You are in my thoughts, my prayers and my heart. So keep reaching for the "brass ring" and ride this merry-go-round we call life. It's pretty awesome, as are you! Sent with huge bear hugs and lots of love.

S. W.

July 10th, 2013

Sir, I pray for your comfort and painless days. You are always in my thoughts. Keep strong.

L. K.

July 10th, 2013

Keep aiming, Ken! I admire your strength and I'm with ya! You are in my prayers.

J. K.

July 11th, 2013

You are truly an inspiration, Ken and always have been.

D. S.

July 12th, 2013

I love you!

J. F. F.

August 5th, 2013

Thinking of you always.

J. B.G., D. and M. J. B.

*****

Ken's faithful companion, Poko, passed away on August 9th, 2013.

*****

August 9ᵗʰ, 2013

Sir, I'm so sorry for your loss. Animals are as loyal to us as we are to them. He loved you so much. When the time comes, you and he will be reunited again.

L. K.

August 9ᵗʰ, 2013

We all loved him very much. We love you.

K. and E. K.

August 9ᵗʰ, 2013

My deepest condolences, Ken. I know how difficult it is to loose a fur baby and my heart goes out to you. I always found comfort in printing out a few nice photos.

B. J. O.

August 9ᵗʰ, 2013

Darn you, Ken Kelly! I should not have read this at work! It is so heartbreaking when our loyal four-legged friends die. It leaves a hole in our lives. Having just lost a beloved dog, that pain dulls, but a certain memory or favorite toy found stirs that pain ever so slightly. After I wiped the tears from my eyes, my first thought (honestly) was that I wished I worked for FLA longer so I would have had more memories of the good times working with you! Many blessings to you!

D. T.

August 9ᵗʰ, 2013

I am very sorry for your loss. Cherish the memories and learn from your experiences. May God bless you and your family.

J. B.

August 9ᵗʰ, 2013

Ken and Mickie, my heart is with you both.

R. S.

August 15ᵗʰ, 2013

Ken, I recently lost a Chihuahua that I had for twenty years, so I know your pain. She also died in my arms, and I cried for hours and sometimes still do. The only hope or advice I can give is, get another little dog. It will never ever replace the one lost, but it will help to fill in a little bit of the huge hole in your heart.

M. H.

August 22ⁿᵈ, 2013

Ken, hugs to you and Mickie. I saw the plaque you made for your dear friend Poko. It is beautiful. I know as you both sit on your deck and look at it, it will bring joy and sadness at the same time. We love you both.

T. K.

February 9ᵗʰ, 2014

Ken, I don't know if you will be back on here, but you didn't loose your fight with the beast. You control it as long as your body will stay standing. Your mind and your will are amazing to me and all around you. We are so sad that you are in hospice (The Hospeace House in Naples) now. We know soon you will be with the One who made you as the kind, loving, caring, stubborn and very knowledgeable person I know. S. and I, and many others know when you stand before the Lord, He is going to say to you, "*Well done, my son*". Thank you for being a great brother-in-law and for all you have done for everyone in this family, for your friends, the ones you work with and the so, so many people you have trained in the field that you love with your whole heart. You have left a very long list of medics to carry on your great love for caring for people. You will be deeply missed when that time comes. Your love and impact you have had on everyone will be here forever. Our children and grandchildren love you just as much as we do and will miss you. I know we will see you again on the other side.

We love you,
T. and S. K.

*****

Ken Kelly entered into eternity on March 9th, 2014 at the Hospeace House in Naples, New York.
Ken, we will strive to Carpe diem for you. We will strive to Seize the day.

*****

May 28th, 2014

Ken, it is May 28th, 2014, at 4:22 in the morning; and we miss you all so very much. But we are so happy you are in Heaven with Ma, Dad and your brother. We love you!

T. K.

June 19th, 2014

Ken, I know that while your physical body is not here, I know that you are watching over all of your family and friends. As you probably know, I am now a sitting town judge. I credit a lot of that to you and the lessons you taught me over the years. I try to show the patience that you did when dealing with problems.

My friend, you are always in my thoughts and prayers as is your family. Until we meet again, have a great day and enjoy the wonderful weather my friend. I know you liked it warm so that you could ride the bike.

P. H.

July 4th, 2014

I just reconnected with B. K. on Facebook. I kind of wish I didn't, because to me, you were still physically with us. I guess I loved my denial. I've been avoiding asking because I had a feeling you had moved on, Mr. Kelly. I will never forget that great, handsome smile, devil looks and genuine concern for others.

You taught so many of us how to be better on so many levels. I will continue to think of you often.

I passed my nursing boards and joined the "other side" in March, and you were one of the very first ones I thought of. Also, because of you, I've managed to go from a size-56 uniform pant down to a size 40, and I've been under three hundred pounds for seven years now. Thanks for changing my life, Sir.

B. J. O.

About the Author

Ken Kelly had been in Emergency Medical Services since his time as a soldier. He began as an Emergency Medical Technician and worked his career up to be a paramedic and a paramedic instructor and so very much more.

Mickie Kelly became a Licensed Practical Nurse in 1968 and an EMT volunteer in 1988.

Ken began at Finger Lakes Ambulance in Clifton Springs, New York, in late 1993, and Mickie started there in March of 1994 as an EMT/Dispatcher.

Ken and Mickie met, worked together and became friends. That is a love story in itself and they were married on August 28th, 2004.

Ken began his greatest challenge on April 20th, 2009, until his passing on March 9th, 2014.

Mickie continues to be a volunteer EMT and an EMS Lieutenant for Hopewell Fire Department, just east of Canandaigua, New York.

She has learned so very much from this amazing man and will continue to pass on the legacy of his teachings, inspiring thoughts, insights and so very much more.

About the Motorcycle

Ken loved his motorcycle and was well-known for riding it to work, to classes, and just riding it. Finger Lakes Ambulance now has his motorcycle and has dressed it up with emergency lights, a siren, and many special words of wisdom of Ken's. It will be featured in many of the parades in our area.

Please come out and see this awesome reminder of Finger Lakes Ambulance and Ken Kelly's legacy.

Thank you very much,

Mickie Kelly

Printed in the USA
CPSIA information can be obtained
at www.ICGtesting.com
LVHW051634280723
753515LV00001B/21

9 798887 511368